U.S. Department of Justice
Office of Justice Programs
Office of Juvenile Justice and Delinquency Prevention

Juvenile Accountability Incentive
Block Grants Program

January 2000

From the Administrator

"If you build it, they will come" appears to ring true when it comes to the construction of new or expanded juvenile detention facilities. Before embarking on such a costly course of action, however, a community should carefully assess its facility needs and ensure that it is effectively using alternatives to secure confinement when appropriate.

The Juvenile Accountability Incentive Block Grants (JAIBG) program provides assistance in building or expanding juvenile correction and detention facilities and in training correctional staff. This Bulletin, one in a series featuring JAIBG Best Practices, offers helpful information about such key aspects as construction decisions, master planning, facility development, and training. It also provides sources of additional information, including useful publications.

Shay Bilchik
Administrator

Construction, Operations, and Staff Training for Juvenile Confinement Facilities

David Roush and Michael McMillen

This Bulletin is part of OJJDP's Juvenile Accountability Incentive Block Grants (JAIBG) Best Practices Series. The basic premise underlying the JAIBG program, initially funded in fiscal year 1998, is that young people who violate the law need to be held accountable for their offenses if society is to improve the quality of life in the Nation's communities. Holding a juvenile offender "accountable" in the juvenile justice system means that once the juvenile is determined to have committed law-violating behavior, by admission or adjudication, he or she is held responsible for the act through consequences or sanctions, imposed pursuant to law, that are proportionate to the offense. Consequences or sanctions that are applied swiftly, surely, and consistently, and are graduated to provide appropriate and effective responses to varying levels of offense seriousness and offender chronicity, work best in preventing, controlling, and reducing further law violations.

In an effort to help States and units of local government develop programs in the 12 purpose areas established for JAIBG funding, Bulletins in this series are designed to present the most up-to-date knowledge to juvenile justice policymakers, researchers, and practitioners about programs and approaches that hold juvenile offenders accountable for their behavior. An indepth description of the JAIBG program and a list of the 12 program purpose areas appear in the overview Bulletin for this series.

Overview

JAIBG funds may be used to develop programs in any of 12 program purpose areas established by Congress. The first of these areas—"building, expanding, renovating, or operating temporary or permanent juvenile correction or detention facilities, including training of correctional personnel"—addresses construction, operation, and training. Before beginning construction, however, jurisdictions should complete a master plan, determine what type of facility will best meet their needs and expectations, and reach a decision to construct. Master planning is a key component because it establishes the specific policies to prevent and reduce crowding and control the length of stay (DeMuro and Dunlap, 1998).

To provide practitioners practical guidance and advice on best practices under JAIBG Program Purpose Area 1, this paper addresses five main themes: construction decisions, master planning, facility development, operations, and training.

- **Construction decisions.** Construction under Program Purpose Area 1 includes building new facilities, expanding existing capacity through new construction, and renovating existing facilities. There are many reasons to build, including the large number of juveniles currently incarcerated in crowded facilities (Parent et al., 1994), the pressing need for secure beds in jurisdictions without juvenile detention, and the deteriorating condition of many facilities.

  Because construction is expensive, decisions to build, expand, or renovate facilities should be reached by using systematic, data-driven, and rational methods. Decisionmakers, for example, should be able to provide empirical evidence of a need for construction. If data indicate a need to build, then jurisdictions have a strong rationale for construction.

- **Master planning.** Master planning is a systematic process that increases the effectiveness of long-term decisionmaking. Using a team of juvenile justice specialists and planners from outside a jurisdiction, the process leads key juvenile justice and community stakeholders through activities that will elicit a locally defined vision and mission for the jurisdiction's juvenile justice system. Data collection and operational recommendations are then based on these core values and principles.

- **Facility development.** The facility development process, which begins with operational/architectural programming, involves documenting operational priorities and determining spatial requirements and arrangements that will respond to a facility's management, daily

programming, and environmental needs. During facility development and prior to the start of physical design activities, jurisdictions should also define cost parameters for staffing and construction and identify site issues.

- **Operations.** Program Purpose Area 1 includes operations, which for juvenile detention and corrections facilities involves programs and services. Consistent with the competency development aspect of the Balanced and Restorative Justice (BARJ) model,[1] the operation of juvenile facilities rests on the assumption that the best way to improve public safety is by changing an offender's behavior. Success in doing so, however, is people-driven and, therefore, expensive (with staff costs for salaries, benefits, and training constituting a large part of operational costs). To help jurisdictions develop effective operating practices, this Bulletin identifies the fundamental needs of facilities and the key elements of operations, such as organizational prerequisites and program, staffing, and management principles.

- **Staff Training.** Accountability-based interventions change juvenile offenders' behavior by providing them with opportunities to experience positive relationships with healthy adults in appropriate settings. Staff training is the most cost-effective way to integrate accountability-based principles into staff development in juvenile confinement and custody facilities.[2] Staff training technology has expanded greatly

through the programs and services of the American Correctional Association (ACA), the Juvenile Justice Trainers Association (JJTA), the National Institute of Corrections (NIC) Academy Division, the National Juvenile Detention Association (NJDA), the Office of Juvenile Justice and Delinquency Prevention's (OJJDP's) Training and Technical Assistance Division (TTAD), and an increasing number of State-operated training academies. Although this Bulletin presents several training models and resources, it cannot capture all of the abundant knowledge on best practices in this area. Summaries of effective programs, along with a list of resources and an extensive bibliography, are provided to help practitioners retrieve original works and supplemental materials.

Construction Decisions—Assessing the Need To Build

Juvenile detention and corrections have become big business, with more and more jurisdictions spending increasing amounts of time, energy, and money to expand detention and corrections capacity.[3] As public agencies, private organizations, architects, and court systems approach construction more aggressively than ever, more and larger juvenile facilities come off the drawing boards every day in a building surge that has begun to rival the exponential growth of adult facilities in the 1970's and 1980's. Facilities for young people are no longer an

---

[1] The Balanced and Restorative Justice (BARJ) model, a core component of the OJJDP Comprehensive Strategy, is a combination of the Balanced Approach and the Restorative Justice models. It includes community protection, offender accountability, offender competency development, and restoration.

[2] Confinement refers to a physically restricting placement, and custody describes places and programs (such as shelter care, day treatment, and home detention) that involve supervision but may allow youth to leave at specified times.

[3] Juvenile detention refers to the custody process that occurs between the time of a juvenile's arrest and the time of his or her adjudication or disposition. It includes a range of placement alternatives that vary in restrictiveness from home detention to secure detention. Correctional placements, by contrast, take place after a juvenile has been adjudicated as an offender and a dispositional plan (or sentence) has been determined. Correctional placement alternatives range from small and open residential settings to large, State-operated, maximum-security corrections facilities. Some jurisdictions allow the dispositional placement of juveniles in detention facilities, an action that complicates the distinction between detention and corrections.

afterthought, buried in the recesses of civic concern and public budgets; they are "big-ticket" items occupying communities' full and serious attention.

Reasons for Construction

Reasons for the recent explosion in construction of juvenile residential facilities are found in both fact and perception. On the factual side, crowding is widespread (Parent et al., 1994), making affected residential programs difficult to manage and not as safe as those operating at recommended capacities. Residents spend more time in lockdown, and program quality suffers (Previte, 1997). When staff must focus primarily on safety and security, effective intervention and treatment are compromised. In addition, because staffing levels rarely increase as quickly as the number of residents, crowded facilities often do not have enough staff to do the job well.

Another reason for the recent growth in construction is the large number of aging and outdated physical plants, many built during the construction booms following World War II (see Norman, 1961). Facilities built during the 1950's, 1960's, and 1970's are fast approaching the end of their useful lifespan, an end brought nearer by the ravages of crowding and (for many facilities) inadequate maintenance and repair budgets. Such older facilities also were never intended to withstand the intense uses they now frequently must serve. While juvenile facilities once served a largely non-violent and manageable population (with few serious offenders), they now serve juveniles with profound behavioral problems and learning deficits and significant mental health needs, many of whom present security problems (Cocozza, 1992; Otto et al., 1992). A large number of facilities are inappropriately configured to meet these needs.

A need for increased capacity is another factor driving construction. Until recently, jurisdictions nationwide have experienced an increase in juvenile arrests overall and in arrests for increasingly serious offenses. In communities that have their own secure facilities, the increase has caused buildings to become crowded and/or juveniles to be turned away. Jurisdictions that rely on other communities for secure beds are frequently told that no room is available. In both situations, one immediate solution has been to construct new bed space. With more beds, communities reason, there will be no crowding, operations will improve, and problems will go away.

In many instances, communities have been correct in perceiving a need for added capacity. For example, in jurisdictions where population has doubled or tripled over the past 20 years (often with accompanying changes in juvenile offenders and in the general social fabric), institutional capacities may now be totally inadequate. In many communities, especially those where juvenile court placement practices have not changed, comprehensive master planning has confirmed a need for additional capacity to respond to current and future needs. In other communities, however, studies have shown that juvenile facilities are housing youth who pose no significant threat to community safety or the court process and who could be managed as effectively in less restrictive and less costly programs and settings (Boersema, 1998; Boersema et al., 1997; Jones and Krisberg, 1994). In these instances, the perception that secure custody is necessary for all juveniles being detained (and perhaps many more) conflicts with the reality. When placement in a secure facility is a jurisdiction's primary or only treatment option, it becomes an expensive catchall, one that replaces less restrictive and equally (or more) appropriate alternatives (Dunlap and Roush, 1995).

Alternatives to Construction

When the perceived need for added capacity conflicts with reality, a business-as-usual approach to secure custody generates high bed-need projections, which, in turn, result in excess capacity. Excess capacity then leads to continued overuse of secure custody for juveniles and an immediate and lasting strain on financial resources. A jurisdiction may build its way out of problems, but only temporarily. The numbers usually catch up with the space available—and usually more quickly than anyone expected.

In response to these concerns, many jurisdictions are pursuing alternatives to construction. This approach, which uses a range of variably restrictive residential and nonresidential services, is commonly called "the continuum of care." Similar to the graduated sanctions model set forth in OJJDP's *Comprehensive Strategy for Serious, Violent, and Chronic Juvenile Offenders* (Wilson and Howell, 1993), the continuum-of-care approach requires jurisdictions to examine closely how to direct resources toward managing public safety and meeting the needs of the greatest number of juveniles (Bilchik, 1998). The continuum-of-care approach commonly considers and implements a variety of services (such as home detention, electronic monitoring, afterschool and evening report programs, day treatment, restitution, shelter care, and staff-secure residential programs) as alternatives to physically restrictive detention custody (DeMuro, 1997; Guarino-Ghezzi and Loughran, 1996; Howell, 1997).

The JAIBG program raises two important questions related to maintaining a strong continuum of services. First, given JAIBG's endorsement of the concept of graduated sanctions, will jurisdictions develop and expand the range of sanctions to serve as consequences for delinquency? Second, will an overreliance on juvenile institutions as a first or primary sanction occur that will weaken other sanctions or the continuum itself? The development of a strong continuum of services would seem to help achieve JAIBG's goal of having sanctions that are graduated, immediate, and accountability oriented. In addition, a strong continuum may address many jurisdictions' lack of dispositional options (sanctions) between probation and incarceration. By providing juvenile court judges with options, a strong continuum of care will improve the juvenile justice system's ability to deliver appropriate sanctions and hold offenders accountable.

Master Planning—Getting the Numbers Right

In those instances when increased capacity is necessary, deciding to build a new facility is only the first of many difficult and critical decisions that a jurisdiction must make. Because physical facilities exist for a long time, jurisdictions should make every effort to ensure that the process leading to construction will produce the best and most appropriate buildings possible.

Master planning is the most important step in the construction process (Elias and Ricci, 1997; Farbstein/Williams and Associates, 1981; Kimme et al., 1988; McMillen and Hill, 1997). Juvenile justice system literature emphasizes the importance of using planning models to make responsible decisions about bed space and construction needs (Boersema, 1998; DeMuro, 1997; Jones and Steinhart, 1994). Chinn (1996) outlines a planning strategy to find new solutions for housing habitually violent young offenders. The National Center for Juvenile Justice recommends a 10-step master planning process to address a range of problems (Steenson and Thomas, 1997); and Barton (1994), Guarino-Ghezzi and Loughran (1996), and Schwartz (1994) commend the steps in the master planning process as a strategy to effect broad systems reform. NIC conducts Planning of New Institutions (PONI) workshops and provides materials that address the construction

planning process (National Clearinghouse for Criminal Justice Planning and Architecture, 1996; Taylor et al., 1996; Voorhis, 1996). PONI workshops for juvenile institutions are currently available to juvenile justice practitioners.

Responding to crowding and a need for less restrictive services, NJDA assembled teams of planners, architects, juvenile justice systems specialists, and law enforcement specialists to develop juvenile justice master plans for several judicial circuits in Illinois (Boersema, 1998). In each circuit, teams considered how many secure detention beds would be needed in the future and developed master plans with a wide range of alternatives, including construction of secure and staff-secure detention beds.[4] Even though the jurisdictions described themselves as very similar to one another, the planning process revealed significant differences to key stakeholders. Given these differences, the assumption that "one size fits all" can be misleading and costly — especially when the proposed solution requires construction of new secure beds.

The master planning process can change a jurisdiction's understanding of its needs, including the size of the facility it thinks that it needs (McMillen, 1998). In one jurisdiction, for example, a review of intake decisions prompted the chief juvenile court judge and circuit court administrator to modify the intake process for all juvenile justice system components, including law enforcement. This change led to an immediate and lasting 40-percent drop in the detention facility's average daily population. Intake data not previously considered also allowed the jurisdiction to lower its bed-space projections. Given serious structural problems with the existing facility,

---

[4] The term "staff-secure" refers to security resulting from the presence of and measures taken by staff members, rather than conditions created by the presence of locks or other hardware.

the final recommendation was to build a new secure detention center with a capacity that was 10 beds higher than that of the existing facility. The jurisdiction's initial request, by contrast, had been to construct a facility with almost twice the number of new beds actually needed. Without a systematic assessment by individuals outside the system, the jurisdiction would have significantly overbuilt.

Planning Team Members

Given the high cost of juvenile facility construction, a jurisdiction should carefully review the qualifications of master planning team members and make sure that the team includes the following: an architect experienced in building juvenile facilities, a planner with juvenile justice and master planning experience who is knowledgeable in data collection and analysis procedures, a juvenile justice systems specialist experienced in operating model or effective programs and services, and a local law enforcement specialist who can provide access to information and services from local law enforcement agencies.

Planning Steps

Jurisdictions assessing space needs should complete the following important planning steps:

Step 1: Form an advisory group

Each jurisdiction should form an advisory group to guide planning efforts. Whether called a stakeholders group, steering committee, community advisory group, or interagency workgroup, the group should include the jurisdiction's chief probation officer; its superintendent(s) of juvenile confinement facilities; responsible local juvenile justice advocates; and representatives from the juvenile court, local law enforcement, the public defender's and prosecutor's offices, youth-serving agencies, placement agencies for adjudicated youth, and community organizations (DeMuro and Dunlap, 1998).

Step 2: Define advisory group tasks

The community advisory group's main tasks are establishing goals for the planning process and monitoring progress toward those goals (Ricci, 1995). Establishing goals involves agreeing on those goals that will appear in a local juvenile justice system's vision and mission statements and identifying the objectives, policies, procedures, and practices related to those goals. Monitoring goals involves considering how critical decisions and outcomes will affect all stakeholders in the system. Careful monitoring will keep decisionmaking balanced and provide the accountability needed to ensure that the process remains consistent with a group's vision and mission statements.

Step 3: Collect and analyze data

Advisory groups should use data collection and analysis resources from both within and outside their jurisdictions. Although local data experts may be familiar with local systems and sources of information, consultants from outside the area may possess broader knowledge of the quality and implications of data and various analysis strategies. The planning team will oversee the data collection process, but the community advisory group should determine the quantity and quality of data to be collected. Because many jurisdictions have inadequate information management systems and important data may be hard to access or of poor quality, data collection and analysis are often tedious steps in the master planning process. To address these obstacles, advisory groups should include data collection procedures in the initial plan.

Data analysis should encompass the full range of services and programs available in the jurisdiction. According to the National Association of Counties (NACO), a jurisdiction's continuum of care may suffer when a new facility is built (Office of Juvenile Justice and Delinquency Prevention, 1998). In jurisdictions with limited resources, a new facility can become a financial drain, leaving fewer resources for alternatives (noninstitutional) and prevention programs.

Schwartz (1994) opposes the use of architects or architectural planning firms to collect and analyze data because a potential conflict of interest between an architect's financial interests and a jurisdiction's best interests may exist when a large construction project is involved. Other practitioners, however, cite examples of architectural planning firms that have completed master plans and advised jurisdictions against building juvenile confinement facilities even when construction would have benefited the firms financially.

Step 4: Obtain technical assistance

Technical assistance regarding how to create a master plan and assess a jurisdiction's need for new or expanded facility construction is available through OJJDP and other sources listed in the "For Further Information" section of this Bulletin.

Step 5: Involve staff

Planning teams and advisory groups should involve facility staff, particularly line staff and first-level supervisors, in the master planning process (Taylor et al., 1996). Experience indicates that youth can also play an important role.

Facility Development— Determining the Type of Facility Needed

For a secure juvenile facility to work well, it must first and foremost be a safe place. Residents should be able to leave and the public enter only at staff's discretion. The facility must be easy to manage, supervise, and maintain, and it must resist the hard use—and at times abuse—of the young people who reside there. It needs adequate space for required and desired programs and services. The space must be arranged in a way that allows staff to do their jobs and residents to do what is required of them in a flexible manner.

A review of plans and programs for juvenile facilities reveals a variety of physical and operational approaches. The approach chosen depends on a community's circumstances and attitudes. Architects generally try to be responsive to both the specific needs of their clients and the constraints imposed by budgets and sites.

Unfortunately, many facilities are designed without information on the specific expectations and needs of those who will use and manage the buildings. In these instances, designers may propose physical structures based on available juvenile or adult system models, which may or may not be appropriate. Without carefully considering the following factors, jurisdictions will be unable to determine the best possible approach for the physical design of their facilities:

- Diverse methods of managing juvenile behavior.
- Resident and staff responses to the physical environment.
- Daily program structure.
- Staffing patterns and costs.
- Circulation and space-sharing patterns in a facility.
- Responses to emergencies and other situations.

Considering these factors may lead planners to discover that a proposed design provides security but fails to achieve other essential goals. Because a successful design is based on the operational priorities of a particular project, rote design (i.e., one that proceeds without considering such priorities) will only compromise a project's goals and ultimate effectiveness.

There is no magical "best approach" to facility design. In developing any new or expanded facility, jurisdictions and their planners must find their own best approach, basing designs on their own expectations, rather than on preconceived architectural notions. The architectural/operational programming process described below permits such an individualized approach.

Architectural/Operational Programming

With growing demands for improved security, program quality, and architectural sophistication, predesign planning has become increasingly important. Operational programming — which should involve key agency and community decisionmakers, court representatives, service providers, and other community stakeholders — involves having these parties examine closely what they intend to accomplish with a proposed facility. Failure to involve all concerned parties in the process can lead to confusion and dissension.

The operational programming process typically begins with a review of a facility's proposed vision and mission statements (e.g., to protect the public and prevent flight from prosecution, provide a safe and secure environment, deliver programming and services consistent with legal requirements, and ensure resident health and welfare). These statements may serve as the foundation for building a hierarchy of programs and spaces. In many cases, however, the statements only begin to scratch the surface of expectations for a facility.

A comprehensive range of philosophical and operational imperatives should be established before physical planning activities begin. Such imperatives may include:

- Implementing behavior management methods.

- Respecting juvenile rights and recognizing juvenile needs.

- Providing programs that address juvenile, system, and family needs.

- Implementing methods for fostering resident accountability, cooperation, and participation.

- Recognizing the importance of resident skills assessment and development.

- Recognizing the importance of family involvement with residents.

- Emphasizing effective intervention and treatment or punishment.

- Appreciating and responding to resident gender, culture, religion, and ethnicity.

- Recognizing the value of links to community and transition services.

- Emphasizing the importance of returning juveniles to productive roles in the community.

These factors, among others, should guide the continuing development and refinement of programs, staffing patterns, environmental quality, and spaces at a proposed facility. If a facility and its services are to succeed, planners should address the use of space only after all other priorities have been established.

Next, operational programming should investigate the following specific issues:

- Security and supervision methods.

- Optimal residential group size for housing and activities.

- Classification.

- Special needs groups.

- Scope of daily programs and services.

- Scheduling of activities.

- Visual/physical connections between activities.

- Resident circulation and movement.

- Environmental priorities (sound, lighting, furnishings, appearance, image).

- Maintenance and repair (durability, life cycle costs).

- Staff communications and support.

- Potential staffing requirements and costs.

- Staff qualifications and training requirements.

- Codes and standards requirements.

- Operational flexibility.

- Future expansion potential.

- Construction cost parameters.

A review of these specific issues will help to determine a facility's essential operational concepts and identify developmental options that are responsive to these essential concepts.

Following close on the heels of operational programming, architectural planning takes all of the previously assembled information and begins to enter real numbers and specific spaces into the equation.

Once a facility's major functions have been identified, the architectural planning process examines the various activities that take place in different areas, the number of people involved, and the times these activities occur. This analysis generates net area (square footage) requirements for anticipated activities. Net area requirements are then combined with circulation and other requirements related to resident and staff movement within the building, the need for other spaces (mechanical rooms, electrical closets, and various undefined spaces), and additional space required for wall thickness and other structural elements. This calculation yields the gross building area or total square footage required for the building. It is not unusual for the total square footage required by a residential facility to be up to 50-percent greater than the net area required for actual user activities.

While individual space requirements for facility functions are being developed (see table 1), architects should explore with facility operators factors—scheduling, potential circulation patterns, supervision and staffing requirements, and options for connecting various spaces and activity zones—to be considered in determining spatial arrangements. Architects should then develop construction diagrams that show the most efficient visual and physical connections (functional adjacencies) and indicate access control points and circulation patterns (see figure 1, page 8).

A facility's design can succeed only to the extent that it meets the needs and expectations of its users. Building a residential facility is expensive and, once construction begins, there is generally no chance to correct errors in design. Comprehensive operational programming and architectural planning provide facility planners with an opportunity to make the best possible decisions from the outset, before committing plans to brick and mortar.

Space Considerations

Defining the gross building area and general spatial arrangements makes it possible to project capital construction costs and related expenditures for furnishings, fees, and site work. Because these projections may form the basis for funding procurement and for ensuring that a building is constructed within budget, the related analysis of space considerations must be thorough. The process of examining space considerations and projecting costs must precede physical design efforts to ensure that all operational objectives are achieved and to prevent costly changes in scope during subsequent design phases (DeWitt, 1987).

The amount of space required for various facility functions depends on many factors, including State licensing and building codes, professional standards of practice (American Correctional Association, 1991a, 1991b, 1991c), and the operational priorities and methods governing where, when, and how activities are to take place. Operational factors should be given high priority because building codes and standards typically do little more than prescribe minimum spatial requirements (American Correctional Association, 1991a, 1991b, 1991c). Facility staff may require the flexibility to depart from certain professional standards of practice to fulfill operational needs specific to their own facility.

Although spatial requirements for secure juvenile facilities vary depending on a facility's capacity and scope of activities, these requirements usually include more space per resident than is required in facilities designed for adults. The demand for a high level of service and activity at juvenile facilities—to keep juveniles occupied during the day and to facilitate the intervention process—requires more space.

In facilities with 50 or fewer residents, spatial allocations of 700 to 800 square feet per resident are not uncommon. Larger facilities, which achieve certain economies of scale, may reasonably average 600 to 700 square feet per resident. A design that significantly exceeds these ranges without offering compelling justification may be seen as overly generous. On the other hand, one that provides significantly less space may jeopardize a facility's functionality.

Table 1: Sample Space Listing (Housing Component)

Space Number	Space/Area	Quantity	Square Feet	Total Net Square Feet	Comments
5.100	Bedrooms (Standard)	9	70	630	Single User, Toilet
5.101	Bedroom (ADA Access)*	1	100	100	Single User, Toilet
5.102	Quiet Living/Dayroom	1	500	500	10 Users, Natural Lighting
5.103	Staff Desk	1	30	30	Open Station, Telephone
5.104	Restroom/Shower	1	70	70	Single User, ADA Access
5.105	Shower	1	40	40	Single User
5.106	Storage/Janitor Closet	1	80	80	With Janitor Sink
	Total Net Square Feet			1,450	
	Six Units (60 Beds) @ 1,450 NSF/Unit			8,700	

Note: Space Listing covers general population housing units with 10 beds.
Source: Mike McMillen, AIA
* Bedroom must be accessible according to standards of the Americans With Disabilities Act (ADA).

Figure 1: Sample Spatial Relationships Diagram

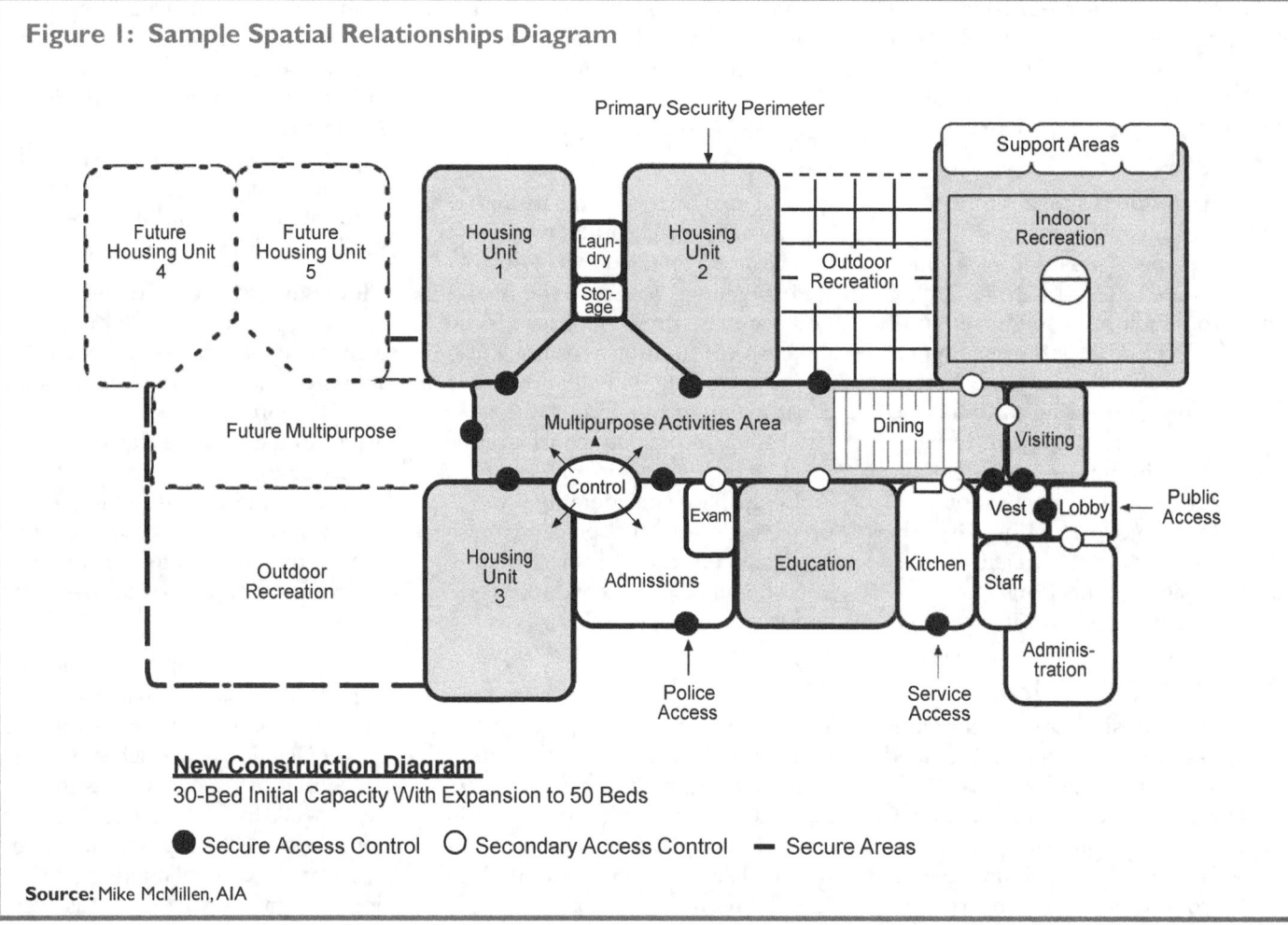

New Construction Diagram
30-Bed Initial Capacity With Expansion to 50 Beds

● Secure Access Control   ○ Secondary Access Control   — Secure Areas

Source: Mike McMillen, AIA

Design Issues

An effective juvenile facility, through a combination of spaces, security features, and environment, allows staff to perform their jobs with ease and professionalism. Although operating an effective residential program for juveniles is never easy, the physical setting can help or hinder operations. If staff members have to struggle with a building to accomplish their objectives, they may not make the effort to do their jobs well or they may seek easier but less beneficial ways to perform their duties. In addition, a building with design elements that provoke undesired responses from residents will only make staff members' jobs harder.

Although no single combination of spaces, security features, and environment is appropriate for every situation, certain aspects of secure residential design are of universal importance. These aspects are discussed below.

Security and safety

Having a secure and safe facility—the first requisite in secure juvenile confinement—involves more than construction materials and hardware. True security and safety derive from a combination of physical materials, management methods, resident supervision, program features, staff support, and access control.

A sharp philosophical shift in the planning and design of juvenile facilities has followed the general trend toward tougher penalties on juvenile offenders (Niedringhous and Goedert, 1998). New juvenile correctional facilities are larger, better equipped with security hardware and technology, and better able to accommodate growth. They also emphasize the use of materials that resist abuse, destruction, and penetration by residents. Although materials that create a less restrictive environment may be available, using durable materials is a way to ensure that a building provides a first line of defense that staff do not need to worry about. If juveniles cannot escape or engage in damaging behavior as a way to exert control or gain attention, then both staff and residents will be able to focus on more productive activities.

Most new facilities feature a secure building perimeter that minimizes the potential for unauthorized resident egress, public access, and resident contact with the public. Within the building, major functional spaces such as housing, education, recreation, dining, and visiting areas are zoned so that staff can control resident access and maintain appropriate group size and separation. Many facilities control access between zones remotely (from a central security or control station), making it unnecessary for staff to carry keys (often a target of residents). To ensure continuous visual contact between residents and staff, walls of damage-resistant glazing are used extensively in partitions separating residential areas. Nearly all housing in new facilities consists of single-occupancy bedrooms with integral sanitary fixtures.

If these features seem like those already common in adult facilities, there is good reason. Juvenile justice practitioners today face many of the same safety and security problems that their adult system counterparts have long faced, making a similar level of protection necessary in juvenile facilities. In many ways, however, differences between juvenile and adult operations are more pronounced now than in the past.

Direct supervision

Direct supervision in adult corrections (Farbstein, Liebert, and Sigurdson, 1996; Nelson, 1993; Nelson et al., 1984) is not the same as direct supervision in juvenile facilities. The staffing ratio is one source of difference. Adult facilities commonly use 1 correctional officer for every 40 or more inmates (Nelson et al., 1984; Wright and Goodstein, 1989). To maintain safety and security with this ratio, adult facilities rely on electronic surveillance, security construction, and behavior management teams or therapeutic Special Weapons and Tactics (SWAT) teams charged with crisis management. By contrast, juvenile facilities usually need 1 staff person working directly with every 8 to 10

juveniles to ensure effective involvement and behavior management. (Having 1 staff member supervise 40 juveniles would be a prescription for serious problems.) In addition, almost all juvenile facilities use direct supervision staffing patterns, with staff physically present and directly involved with residents at all times. Juveniles are not (and should not be) left to their own devices or managed by remote control.

Higher staff-resident ratios at juvenile facilities allow for more effective interaction. When staff have many opportunities to work with residents, problems can be identified and resolved before they pose a threat to safety. Juveniles themselves will feel safer, will feel less exposed to unknown threats, and will be less likely to act out.

Another common and effective supervision strategy at juvenile facilities is having residents participate regularly in programs and services such as education, recreation, and counseling. A juvenile who is occupied and engaged is far less likely to present behavior problems. He or she will also realize general benefits in such areas as personal skills development, health maintenance, academic achievement, and cooperation (Glick and Goldstein, 1995; Henggeler, 1998; Rubenstein, 1991).

Normalization of the residential environment—both the physical and operational character of a facility—is another essential element in developing a safe and secure setting. Although a secure detention facility is not an environment that most residents would describe as normal, many facilities today are designed with the intent of minimizing overtly institutional characteristics so that residents will not engage in the negative behaviors that an institutional environment may prompt. Spatial variety, movable furnishings, natural lighting, acoustic control, housing/group size, and opportunities for resident movement are design elements that can help to reduce the sense of

crowding and restrictiveness that often leads residents to engage in thoughtless and unsafe behavior.

Despite the need for increasingly restrictive physical features, juvenile justice professionals continue to emphasize the need for facilities to reflect intense concern for the juveniles who reside in them. For example, professionals demand buildings that support a wide range of activities and encourage ongoing contact between residents and staff. In this context, security and safety are recognized as necessary to accommodate people and places— rather than as ways to create coercive and restrictive confinement.

Group size/classification

Another fundamental difference between juvenile and adult facilities is the typical size of resident groups or housing units. Although housing units with capacities of 25 to 40 are common at adult facilities, juvenile facilities rarely have units that house more than 12 to 16 residents and often have units that house as few as 8 residents. Juvenile programs avoid larger resident groups for various reasons, including the following:

- Larger groups of juveniles are more difficult to manage.

- It is harder for staff (who are often both counselors and supervisors) to work effectively with individuals in larger groups.

- It is more difficult to move larger groups for various program activities.

An increasingly important reason for small group sizes at juvenile facilities relates to resident classification priorities. In the past, most juvenile facilities had relatively small capacities. These small facilities needed small resident groups in order to separate boys from girls and older youth from younger and to make it possible for staff to work with residents on a more individualized basis. Today, juvenile facilities are becoming larger, but the need for more refined classification methods (and for the ability to place residents in small groups) is more apparent than ever. Juvenile facilities are receiving a higher percentage of serious offenders, sexual offenders, juveniles with identified substance abuse and mental health problems, and female offenders. Accordingly, facilities need something other than a one-size-fits-all management approach. They need an approach that includes specially structured programming and services and the ability to classify and separate juveniles into small groups for housing and program purposes. Although program staff rarely, if ever, want to assemble large groups of juveniles, they should be able to do so when necessary or appropriate without being restricted by the organization or spatial limitations of a building.

The issue of what housing unit size is best has by no means been resolved and probably never will be. Economic considerations (smaller units usually mean higher staffing costs) often conflict with operational needs (smaller units can mean better staff management of residents). Therefore, different balances must be struck in different communities. Although most programs call for smaller units (up to 12 residents), some prefer larger units with multiple staff assigned to each unit to allow staff present to provide immediate support. Some jurisdictions insist on making all housing units in a single facility the same size, thereby permitting consistent and efficient staff allocation (because it is virtually impossible to predict how the number of residents in each classification will change over time). Others require the development of variable-size housing units so that certain groups of residents can be lodged in smaller groups, based on management and program needs. Although there is more than one way of doing things correctly, juvenile facilities generally lean toward smaller

group sizes and staffing levels that support this approach.

Environmental concerns

The wisdom of Vitruvius (the Greek scholar who explained that a building may be judged by its adherence to the principles of commodity, firmness, and delight) has certain relevance to environmental concerns that are pertinent to juvenile facilities. By commodity, Vitruvius meant that a building must serve the function for which it was intended. By firmness, he meant that a building should be able to withstand the rigors of wind, rain, and inhabitants. By delight, he meant that a building should provide enjoyment to its users.

Although it is easy to see how the concepts of commodity and firmness apply to secure juvenile facilities, it is harder to see the connection between secure juvenile facilities and the principle of delight. The concept of delight, however, applies in many ways to these facilities. The spaces that people live and work in profoundly affect their attitudes, comfort levels, and feelings about how good or bad their circumstances are. In turn, these perceptions influence people's approaches to getting through each day. A person in an inhospitable, threatening, or demeaning environment, for example, may feel overcome by circumstances and seek relief through isolation. A person in a restrictive environment might try to exert control over his or her situation by attempting to change things or simply trying to get up and leave.

In a secure juvenile facility, none of these responses is desirable. Juveniles who isolate themselves (emotionally or physically) become unreachable and pose special management problems. Juveniles who try to exert control through aggressive, confrontational, or manipulative behavior present a danger to staff and other residents and disrupt the smooth flow of daily activities. Although

leaving a secure custodial setting is not an option for residents, the possibility that they will plot such an action is a continuing source of staff concern.

Some secure residential facilities for juveniles are designed to inhibit or prevent these undesirable responses by physically restricting residents at all times and using materials and spaces that allow no opportunity for entry or escape. Such buildings, however, often evidence little consideration for the sensibilities of their occupants. At the opposite extreme, other buildings are completely nonrestrictive and are designed for management methods that rely entirely on staff and program structure to respond to and control any potential problem behaviors.

The majority of juvenile facilities fall somewhere in between these extremes, depending on the population being served and local attitudes. Most are designed both to be physically durable and to take human factors into account. Providing residents opportunities to cooperate and behave responsibly encourages them to do so and to become more accountable for their actions. The physical setting, while discouraging abuse or destruction of the building and its furnishings by residents, must also project an image that reinforces society's positive expectations of juveniles (rather than one that will provoke counterproductive responses).

Such a setting offers a normalized or noninstitutional environment, one whose features will moderate the perception of institutional confinement. Small group living arrangements relieve the sense of crowding and the strain of fitting in with other youth. Natural lighting and regular physical and visual access to outdoor spaces reduce impressions of confinement, as does the ability to move among locations with varied spatial character. A quiet acoustic environment, achieved through carpeting and other surface treatments, furnishings, and spatial configurations, can be used to create the perception of a calm and controlled setting.

In a 1998 keynote address to the American Institute of Architects Conference, James Bell, a staff attorney for the Youth Law Center, described the optimal features of a juvenile facility as follows:

> While technology may be good for adult incarceration, it has proven repeatedly to be a poor way to administer juvenile facilities. Use your designs as a tool to try to reduce warehousing of young people, many of whom have still not been adjudicated delinquent.
>
> Make sure there is plenty of light and space. Juveniles in general are mercurial, and they definitely are so while detained. A light, spacious setting can improve their spirits when they return from court or from a visit that goes poorly.
>
> Make sure there is enough space for large muscle exercise and for classrooms and contact visiting. Be wary of multiple use rooms that are supposed to serve as the primary classroom. You can believe that any space not designated specifically for classrooms will probably not be used as such. There are too many competing needs for any large space and school will be one of the first casualties.
>
> I know that you can design facilities that downplay the negative aspects of confinement and provide positive space through your use of natural light, glass, colors, textures, and furnishings.

Staff support, communication, and supervision

One of the great challenges in developing effective operations and management practices in a juvenile facility is the need for staff to work consistently and effectively with residents. To do so, staff must be confident of both their personal safety and the overall security of the facility. When staff are responsible for too many residents, when they doubt the availability of assistance in emergencies, or when they have a limited number of responses to resident behavior, they are likely to avoid close contact with residents under their care and rely on physically restrictive measures to achieve control. As a result, program quality suffers, and a more institutional character prevails.

Appropriate group size is a decisive factor in staff members' perception of control. The ability to keep groups within various zones also contributes to a sense of control. Other design features affect staff perception of control. Housing and activity spaces, for example, should be arranged in a way that promotes a high degree of visibility for staff within and outside those areas. Juveniles should not be able to conceal themselves in corners or rooms that are not directly supervised. Resident circulation between physically controlled security zones (housing, education, recreation, visiting, dining) should also be direct and easily observed by staff. Residents should know that they are being observed at all times and that there are no gaps in surveillance—even when staff are not working with them directly. Remote audio and visual monitoring systems should be used, as appropriate, to supplement direct supervision and to ensure backup during periods of low staffing.

Staff members must also be able to communicate immediately with one another at all times. Access to audio communication systems should be uncomplicated and widely available. In many new facilities, staff are equipped with cordless telephones or other wireless communication devices to ensure instant connection to other staff and prompt notification of others in the event of an emergency.

Housing

Housing is a critical issue in designing a successful juvenile facility. As discussed above (under "Group size/classification"), housing units for juveniles tend to be smaller than those in adult facilities. The vast majority of units in juvenile facilities support 8 to 12 residents—the maximum number, according to juvenile authorities, that a single staff person can manage effectively with a high level of staff interaction and safety (Parent et al., 1994). Although smaller units may result in less efficient staffing patterns, they may be necessary for certain categories of offenders. Larger housing units—though more common in recent large facilities—are generally considered unacceptable in small facilities because it is harder to classify residents when they are part of larger groups.

Housing units must support such varied activities as sleeping, counseling, studying, reading, writing, playing board games, using a computer, and watching television. Staff generally want housing areas to be quiet spaces that provide residents with a sense of calm, reflection, and privacy after days filled with structured programs and activities. To control noise and intensity levels, active pursuits such as table games, exercise, and recreation often occur outside of, but close to, housing areas.

To create spatial flexibility and allow for certain program activities in housing areas, many housing unit designs include living space beyond the minimum levels required by national standards. Many facilities also now incorporate easily accessible activity spaces, both indoor and outdoor, in close proximity to housing.

Some new facilities feature housing units based on the "unit management concept," meaning that the majority of resident activities (including dining and education) occur within the housing unit. This approach minimizes resident circulation. Most residential programs, however, involve extensive movement of residents among spaces and reserve housing units for sleeping, studying, and engaging in certain small group activities. Although either approach can be successful, the decision to pursue one over the other should be carefully considered during project planning phases because the two approaches require radically different designs.

Regardless of the amount of resident movement envisioned, most housing areas in new juvenile facilities include the following:

- Single-occupancy sleeping rooms.
- Group living spaces.
- Individual showers and restrooms.
- Storage spaces for clothes, linens, and other items used on the unit.
- Accessible janitor closets (which facilitate resident participation in cleaning).

Staff desk areas are often included in housing areas to allow staff members to complete paperwork and related activities in close proximity to residents. According to the mandates of the 1990 Americans With Disabilities Act, housing unit designs must also now include a certain number of bedrooms with wheelchair access. Many housing units and the areas within and immediately adjacent to them also have laundry facilities that allow resident participation, interview rooms that may be used by social services and other staff members, additional storage space, and "timeout" rooms that permit temporary separation of residents who are exhibiting disruptive behavior.

Single-occupancy sleeping rooms are preferred in most juvenile confinement settings. Although professional standards and case law permit the use of multiple-occupancy sleeping rooms, practitioners have found that shared sleeping spaces—even with intensive supervision—are often a source of increased juvenile injuries, intimidation, and other undesirable behaviors. ACA standards require facilities' living units to be designed primarily for single-occupancy sleeping, allowing no more than 20 percent of housing capacity to be multiple-occupancy sleeping rooms (American Correctional Association, 1991a, 1991b, 1991c). The court in *T.I. et al.* v. *Delia et al.* (King County, WA), for example, held that having three or more youth in one sleeping room constituted a potentially dangerous, and even unconstitutional, threat to individual safety and ordered a stop to multiple-occupancy sleeping rooms (i.e., those with three or more residents) in juvenile detention facilities (cf., Puritz and Scali, 1998).

OJJDP's Research Report *Conditions of Confinement: Juvenile Detention and Corrections Facilities* (Parent et al., 1994) has similarly linked increased juvenile-on-juvenile injuries to large dormitories (11 or more residents in one large room) and recommends eliminating dormitory sleeping arrangements in all juvenile facilities. Because of these concerns, many program operators faced with crowding refuse to place more than one resident in a sleeping room, opting instead to put extra mattresses in separate and easily supervised dayrooms or hallways to minimize the potential for injury or other dangers.

Because sleeping rooms are the hardest areas to supervise, they should be a facility's most durable and abuse-resistant spaces. Hard finishes and stainless steel sanitary fixtures are commonly used, windows and frames are designed to be durable, and windows are designed and located to prevent external communication. Sleeping rooms should include audio communications systems to allow residents to contact staff and staff to contact and monitor residents as necessary. Doors, whether made of heavy-gauge metal or solid wood, should have vision panels. Although fire safety regulations may require remote release doors, normal operations usually allow staff to control sleeping room doors with a key.

Suicide prevention is a paramount concern in designing facilities. The time that a juvenile spends in his or her room, when contact with staff and other residents is limited, can be the most emotionally disturbing period of the juvenile's entire incarceration (Hayes, 1998; Rowan, 1989). Recognizing the potential for suicidal and other dangerous behavior, most residential programs seek to minimize the time that juveniles spend in their rooms. In addition, programs attempt to eliminate protrusions and sharp edges in sleeping rooms and limit residents' access to hardware or other materials that might be used for self-destructive purposes. Sleeping rooms today are consequently more spartan than in the past, an environmental tradeoff considered acceptable given the need for increased safety and the limited time that residents spend there. By contrast, group living spaces in housing units today are generally more open, less confining, and more easily supervised than in the past.

Most program operators favor single-level housing arrangements over multilevel arrangements because single-level arrangements permit easier access to and better supervision of sleeping rooms. Site restrictions, staffing levels, cost constraints, and other factors, however, sometimes require facilities to consider split-level or two-story housing arrangements, with bedrooms stacked vertically around a common living or dayroom area. Although many newer facilities have used this approach successfully (Dugan, 1998), it poses significant design and operational challenges, including potential difficulties with vertical circulation, resident access, emergency egress, room checks and supervision, and ADA compliance and the potential for behavior problems (e.g., jumping or throwing objects from upper levels).

For the most part, secure detention housing spaces are intended to provide a constant level of physical security and supervision that supports flexible use (based on needs determined by staff). Spatial and material distinctions are less important design considerations than a facility's ability to use housing spaces in a variety of ways that may be modified over time.

Programs and Services

Having a full schedule of programs and services available to residents facilitates effective management of their behavior. Keenly aware that residents may find unproductive or damaging outlets for youthful energy when limited opportunities for positive activity are available, program staff in juvenile facilities believe that structured educational and recreational activities are the best defense against misbehavior (Roush, 1996c).

In addition to their behavior management benefits, program and service opportunities are essential to residents' health and well-being (Bell, 1990, 1992, 1996; National Commission on Correctional Health Care, 1999; Soler et al., 1990). Facilities accordingly allow visitation and provide comprehensive education, recreation, counseling, religious, and medical services (Roush, 1993). Although specific requirements for programs in each of these areas are not always defined, professional standards, case law, and State codes mandate provision of these services (Roush, 1993), and best practices demand something more than a minimalist approach.

Education

Although educational programs may meet the letter of the law by assigning residents a few hours of homework each day or requiring them to complete self-directed learning packets and related activities, program operators usually believe that more extensive academic activities are necessary to meet residents' needs (Leone, Rutherford, and Nelson, 1991; Wolford and Koebel, 1995). The time that a juvenile spends in custody, when educators can have his or her undivided attention, is often described as a "teachable moment," a time when considerable learning can take place (Cavanagh, 1995). Given this opportunity, many residential programs feature hours of year-round educational activities (formal and informal) that focus not only on standard academic subjects, but also on the following:

- Life skills development.

- Communications skills assessment.

- Remedial reading and writing instruction.

- Conflict resolution skills development (including instruction on social skills, anger management, and healthy lifestyles).

- Computer literacy.

- Learning skills assessment.

Daytime learning activities frequently carry over into the evening and may also include counseling and group instruction in subjects such as anger management, peer pressure responses, and substance abuse resistance. A well-founded residential program seeks both to identify problems that may contribute to delinquency and to initiate coordinated educational responses to these problems.

Recreation

Recreation includes such diverse activities as exercise and sports, constructive leisure activities for individuals and groups (e.g., crafts, cards, and board games), intellectual activities (e.g., reading, writing, and problem solving), and certain less active pursuits (e.g, computer games) (Calloway, 1995; Grimm, 1998; Roush, 1996c). Active recreational activities (which involve vigorous competitive and noncompetitive activities) are an essential part of daytime and evening programming (Bell, 1990, 1992, 1996; Soler et al., 1990). The availability of indoor space for these activities allows residents to pursue active exercise regardless of weather conditions. Outdoor recreational opportunities should also be available to relieve the stress of constant indoor confinement. For these, practitioners generally favor easily supervised outdoor areas that are close to housing and indoor activity areas (for easy access) and suitable for small groups.

Visitation

Visitation with family members usually involves scheduled periods for group contact visitation,[5] supplemented by prearranged private visits as appropriate. Most facilities include group visiting rooms and private visiting rooms (for meetings with family and legal counsel) within a building's secure perimeter but outside its primary residential areas. Some program operators oppose bringing visitors into any residential areas, given the possible disruption of programming for juveniles receiving visitors, the need to control contraband, and other safety concerns. Some facilities also have a limited number of noncontact visiting rooms to be used in the rare circumstance when potential harm to residents or visitors is anticipated.

Health care

Most juvenile facilities' medical services include medical screening, regular examinations, sick call, and distribution of medications (Morris, Anderson, and Baker, 1996; National

---

[5] During contact visitation, a detained individual and his or her visitor(s) are in the same area; in noncontact visits, they are separated by safety glass.

Commission on Correctional Health Care, 1999; Owens, 1994). Because they require round-the-clock medical staffing, infirmaries are provided in only the largest facilities. Emergency medical services and ongoing medical supervision are usually provided as needed at designated offsite locations, except in the largest facilities.

Because of the number and diversity of health-related problems experienced by juveniles and the proliferation of medications being administered to juveniles in custody, the availability of regular care and attention by qualified medical professionals has become a matter of increasing concern for juvenile facilities. The expanding scope of medical services needed for juveniles in secure residential custody has resulted in increased space needs. Many facilities also now include health education for juveniles as an integral part of their programs.

Site Selection Issues

Site selection is one of the most perplexing decisions jurisdictions face when developing juvenile residential facilities. Many projects encounter resistance from community members who fear that placing a facility near their homes will make their neighborhoods unsafe and cause property values to plummet. Responses of this nature are inevitable when a project is announced without community input and participation. Community involvement should begin at a project's earliest stages and should include meetings to provide background information and public hearings to respond to citizen concerns. Although involving the community will not guarantee a facility's acceptance, failure to address local concerns publicly and directly will invite conflict.

Unfortunately, the fear of political backlash or community opposition too often prompts planners to select remote sites that are incompatible with operational needs. From a practical planning perspective, site selection should focus on identifying locations that satisfy a range of operational needs, including the following:

- **Public access.** The site should provide convenient access to families, legal counsel, and local agencies that will have contact with residents. It should be easily accessible by private vehicle or public transportation.

- **Adequate land area.** The site should have sufficient space for a facility's initial construction needs and possible future expansion. Adequate space for a buffer between public areas and secure residential areas is also desirable. A site that is too small may necessitate undesirable vertical development and circulation or may limit outdoor recreation capabilities and future expansion potential.

- **Proximity to population served.** Juvenile facilities should be located near the districts from which their populations are drawn. Such proximity ensures convenient access by families. It also helps facilities recruit staff with cultural/ethnic backgrounds similar to those of the residents being confined. Unfortunately, lower property costs for land in remote locations sometimes lead jurisdictions to select sites in areas that pose access and staffing difficulties.

- **Proximity to courts.** For facilities that hold youth prior to adjudication, sites should be close to both the courts and the facilities where youth may be placed after adjudication and disposition. Such proximity will minimize the time that staff and residents need to spend away from the facility and reduce staffing needs and transportation costs.

- **Compatibility of adjacent land uses.** Site selection should focus on locations that support the residential character of intended operations.

Heavily industrialized areas are generally inappropriate, as are areas with traffic volumes that would threaten effective monitoring of a site's perimeter. Excessive noise (for example, from transportation or a nearby commercial enterprise) should also be avoided.

Site selection and land acquisition are often highly politicized processes and may ultimately require compromise. It is difficult to find a site that satisfies all concerns (Ricci, 1995). Unfortunately, some institutions built in remote areas because of economic incentives end up being staffed by underpaid and undertrained individuals who differ culturally and racially from the resident population (Butterfield, 1998; Kearns, 1998). To avoid such situations, planners should make every effort to identify the characteristics of critical concern to operators and address potential obstacles before the site selection process is finalized.

Construction Costs

Almost every jurisdiction contemplating the construction of a new juvenile facility agonizes about the high costs involved. Although there are ways of reducing costs (e.g., through more efficient systems designs of physical plants and buildings), jurisdictions can go only so far in this direction without compromising operational integrity and environmental quality. The costs of juvenile facilities are especially troubling to funding authorities who compare such costs with the significantly lower relative costs (on a per resident basis) of adult facilities. This comparison is unfair, however, because juvenile facilities usually require substantially more square footage per resident.

At present, juvenile facilities that are highly durable and include a full complement of education and recreation areas and associated administrative, admissions, food service, and other support spaces cost an average of $140 to $160 per square foot for the building itself (McMillen, 1998). This amount includes all construction materials, mechanical/electrical systems, security equipment, and hardware. It does not include additional costs for site work, parking, landscaping, architectural/engineering services, or furnishings; nor does it allow for any contingencies during construction (i.e., changes required because of unforeseen circumstances). These additional costs can increase the cost of facility development by 30 to 35 percent (McMillen, 1998). Even higher costs should be anticipated in locations with high construction cost indexes (e.g., large metropolitan areas).

The cost per bed space is also influenced by a facility's size. Small facilities (25 to 50 beds) require support spaces not appreciably smaller than those in larger facilities (50 to 100 beds), which are able to achieve economies of scale. For this reason, small facilities frequently average between 700 and 800 square feet per resident, while larger detention facilities average 600 to 700 square feet per resident. Long-term care facilities frequently provide more space in support of expanded programming options.

Using average costs for construction and development expenses, table 2 provides examples that illustrate total project costs expected for facilities with 40- and 80-bed capacities.

These examples do not by any means encompass the complete range of development costs for juvenile facilities. A review of recent juvenile facility projects, in fact, reveals that costs vary considerably (above and below) those presented in table 2.

Operational Costs

As high as construction costs may be, they represent only a fraction of the costs that a jurisdiction developing expanded detention capacity will have to bear each year during the life of a facility. For example, the authors' experience has shown that staffing expenses—which account for approximately 80 to 85 percent of annual operating expenditures in facilities with a direct supervision staffing pattern—require annual expenditures amounting to about 25 to 27 percent of a facility's total development cost. The percentage is somewhat lower for large facilities and somewhat higher for small facilities. Staffing expenses include all direct supervision, administration, and program and support services staff that most facilities require. When other expenses (food, clothing, supplies, utilities, communications, normal maintenance, travel, training, and related items) are added to staffing expenses, a facility's total annual operating expenditures may approach 30 to 33 percent of the total facility develop-

ment cost. To operate a facility, therefore, jurisdictions must allocate approximately one-third of a building's cost for each year the building remains open. (For example, a facility that costs $10 million to build will cost approximately $3 million to operate each year.)

For a new facility that will be used for at least 30 years, total operating costs over the lifetime of the facility will exceed construction costs by 10 times or more. Expenditures will actually be even higher, because the operating budget described above does not include expenses associated with debt service of initial construction bonds or the cost of the inevitable repair and replacement of structural and mechanical systems over the life of a building.

A physical design based on staffing efficiency—even if it will involve higher construction expenditures—is of utmost importance. In the interest of fiscal responsibility, however, jurisdictions should carefully consider long-term operational costs throughout the planning process. Only by examining all potential operational expenses rigorously will planners achieve the best possible balance of physical design and supervision needs. The high cost of secure operations further underscores the importance of seeking cost-effective detention alternatives that reduce residential capacity needs while providing necessary supervision, management, and system flexibility (Moon, Applegate, and Latessa, 1997).

Juvenile Facility Operations

Fundamental Needs

OJJDP's *Conditions of Confinement* Research Report (Parent et al., 1994) provides a comprehensive analysis of conditions in juvenile confinement facilities. In particular, the study measured facilities' conformance to

---

Table 2: Construction/Development Cost Examples

Cost Factor	40-Bed Capacity	80-Bed Capacity
Total Square Feet/Resident	750	
Cost per Square Foot (1999)	$150	$150
Total Construction Cost	$4,500,000	$7,800,000
Sitework @ ±9.5% of Construction	$427,500	$741,000
Furnishings @ ±5.0% of Construction	$225,000	$390,000
Arch./Eng. Fees @ ±8.5% of Construction	$382,500	$663,000
Contingency @ ±10.0% of Construction	$450,000	$780,000
Total Project Cost	**$5,985,000**	**$10,374,000**
Total Cost per Resident	**$149,625**	**$129,675**

Note: The table does not include financing/bond costs or administrative fees.

46 assessment criteria that reflected existing minimum national and professional standards in 12 areas:

- Living space.
- Health care.
- Food, clothing, and hygiene.
- Living accommodations.
- Security.
- Control of suicidal behavior.
- Inspections and emergency preparedness.
- Education.
- Recreation.
- Treatment services.
- Access to community.
- Limits on staff discretion.

The 12 areas were each placed in 1 of 4 broad categories (basic needs, order and safety, programming, and juvenile rights). The study examined each facility's conformance with the 12 areas of conditions of confinement. The percentage of facilities that conformed to all criteria in any of the 12 areas ranged from 25 to 85 percent, underscoring a disparity in practices and a national need for improved operations.

Some special problems—such as suicidal behavior, injuries to residents, injuries to staff, and lawsuits—were attributable to isolated events. The study found, however, that most operational problems were correlated with pervasive deficiencies in conditions of confinement. To improve such conditions, the study recommended developing performance-based standards for juvenile facilities. Conditions of confinement, however, are only one part of the larger and more complex measure of juvenile facilities commonly referred to as "quality of life." The study's recommendation of performance-based standards resulted from the finding that high levels of compliance with policy-based criteria did not necessarily result

in improved conditions of confinement, suggesting the need for improved standards and different ways to evaluate quality of life.

Key Elements for Operation

JAIBG Program Purpose Area 1 suggests that a new facility's operation should be as efficient as possible. Ideally, the facility should be a best practices program. The idea of starting a program from scratch or building a facility or operation from the ground up appeals to most juvenile justice practitioners largely because it frees them from all of the "baggage" of past practices. Problems arise, however, when practitioners must conceptualize what kind of program they want (i.e., the principles of running an institution) and determine how to make it happen (i.e., the practice of institutional operations or process).

If successful facility operations were easy to develop, more model programs would exist. Although a model program is difficult to develop, there are sufficient resources (knowledge derived from lessons learned and technology derived from best practices) to guide the development of exemplary programs. This section serves as an operations guide, setting forth steps to take, knowledge and resources to acquire, and people to talk to in order to operate an effective facility. In particular, it outlines three categories of information: (1) organizational prerequisites (components that must be in place before program development can occur), (2) program principles to guide operations, and (3) staffing and management principles to guide implementation. The information provided here does not include standards by which to measure or evaluate facility operations. Instead, this section identifies key elements that should be addressed. If any one of these elements is missing or not fully developed, a facility administrator should be prepared to explain why.

Organizational prerequisites

Safety and security. Safety and security are fundamental prerequisites of program development. Programs cannot grow and evolve unless residents and staff are safe and secure— both physically and emotionally. Physical aspects of safety and security include a new facility's design and construction and policies and procedures that control or prevent juveniles' access to contraband and/ or weapons. Emotional safety and security means that residents and staff feel safe from fear or harm.

Order and organization. Organization is the backbone of program development, the structure upon which effective programs are built. Previte (1994) refers to this structure as "The Code" and identifies three components: order, tradition, and discipline.

- *Order* includes a building's neatness and cleanliness, its adherence to a daily routine or schedule, and a feeling—among residents and staff—of knowing what will happen next. To achieve order, an institution must have a clear and comprehensive policy and procedures manual. To develop the manual, facilities should refer to the series of publications on ACA standards (American Correctional Association, 1991a, 1991b, 1991c, 1994), the series' companion works (American Correctional Association, 1987, 1992a, 1992b, 1992c), chapter 7 of the *Desktop Guide to Good Juvenile Detention Practice* (Roush, 1996b), and products from the OJJDP-sponsored Performance-Based Standards Project managed by the Council of Juvenile Correctional Administrators (CJCA).

- *Tradition* includes customs, routines, songs, and other activities unique to a facility. With a new facility, the possibilities for tradition are endless. Traditions need not be large or complicated; they may be as simple as serving chocolate milk at meals or celebrating birthdays with cake and ice cream. The purpose of tradition is to generate an identity within the facility.

- *Discipline,* by identifying appropriate behaviors and correcting inappropriate behaviors, is a facility's method of building character, pride, and integrity. It involves teaching a collectively endorsed set of appropriate behaviors and values for staff and residents. These behaviors and values are explained in greater detail in the discussion of program principles below.

Conditions of confinement. Conditions of confinement, a model of organizational structure based on the Youth Law Center's C.H.A.P.T.E.R.S. model (Soler et al., 1990), identifies eight areas of institutional operations most likely to be targets of litigation. NJDA recommends that facilities use this model to assess their potential liability before developing programs. Each area in the C.H.A.P.T.E.R.S. model is identified below, and sources of information relevant to each area are cited.

- *Classification and Admissions.* Classification systems are explained in detail in Howell (1997) and OJJDP's *Guide for Implementing the Comprehensive Strategy for Serious, Violent, and Chronic Juvenile Offenders* (Howell, 1995a). Information about admissions appears in American Correctional Association, 1987, 1992c; Christy, 1994; and Roush, 1994, 1996c.

- *Medical and Health Care Services.* Although the National Commission on Correctional Health Care (NCCHC) (1999) and ACA (1991a, 1991b, 1991c) both have standards that address medical and healthcare services, NCCHC's are more comprehensive. Additional information on this topic appears in Morris, Anderson, and Baker (1996) and Owens (1994).

- *Access Issues.* These issues concern a confined juvenile's right to have access to information and individuals outside the facility (e.g., through mail, telephone, visitation, and communication with attorneys and the courts). Bell (1990, 1992, 1996) explains these rights and discusses related standards and case law.

- *Programs.* ACA standards again provide guidance and direction. According to Soler et al. (1990), the courts' primary programming interests are recreation and education. Information about recreation is available in the *Desktop Guide* (Roush, 1996b) and Calloway (1995). Developmentally appropriate best practices are found in Barrueta-Clement et al. (1984) and Kostelnik, Soderman, and Whiren (1999), and guidance on correctional education programs is available in the *Desktop Guide* (Roush, 1996b); Gemignani (1994); Hodges, Giuliotti, and Porpotage (1994); Leone, Rutherford, and Nelson (1991); and Wolford and Koebel (1995).

- *Training.* See "Training" section in this Bulletin.

- *Environmental Issues.* ACA standards address these issues, which include compliance with State and local regulations on health, safety, and sanitation.

- *Confinement and Restraints.* Information appears in the ACA standards, the *Desktop Guide* (Roush, 1996b), Mitchell and Varley (1991), and the NCCHC standards (1999).

- *Safety.* The best sources of information on resident safety are Soler et al. (1990), Hayes (1998), Rowan (1989), Parent et al. (1994), the ACA standards, and the *Desktop Guide.*

Staff. Two organizational prerequisites relate to staff. First, through a central personnel office or consultation with personnel specialists, a new facility should develop an effective program for staff recruitment, selection, reten-

tion, training, and development. Staff training and development are addressed in detail later in this Bulletin.

Second, through its policies and procedures, a facility must ensure that it has sufficient staff to sustain programming. This is a controversial issue, because staffing is the single largest cost in a facility's operational budget and because best practices offer no hard-and-fast rules about staffing levels. Staffing levels depend on many factors, including a program's philosophy, the quality of interactions between staff and residents, the education and training levels of staff, and the physical plant. Best practices are typically associated with facilities that have a small number of youth (6–10) under the direct supervision of any one line staff member (Roush, 1997).

Density. Density (the number of people per unit of space in a facility) is a significant factor in the effectiveness of an institutional program (Roush, 1999). When density creates problems in a juvenile facility, the institution is said to be crowded. The best facilities have plans, policies, procedures, or strategies to address crowding (Burrell et al., 1998; Previte, 1997).

Program principles

Successful programs have core principles or assumptions to guide problem solving and decisionmaking. These principles define a program's purpose and content, articulate what an institution hopes to accomplish, and specify the operations that it will use to accomplish its goals. Frequently called core values, program principles are decisions about the type of facility required to accomplish program goals and the number and type of staff members needed to implement the program.

Many different program models address a wide array of offenders and intervention strategies. In completing a master plan, a jurisdiction identifies the characteristics of its juvenile offender population. It then chooses a program model best suited to the offender population. Research into best practices has revealed that the following program components are successful in juvenile detention and corrections:

Effective assessment. The better the match between offender needs and facility programs and services, the greater the likelihood of success. To assess offender needs, a facility must use effective needs assessment strategies (Agee, 1995; Bell, 1996; Howell, 1995b, 1997).

Behavior contracting. The use of behavior contracts with juvenile offenders is effective, especially when contracts focus on changing behaviors associated with criminal acts (Agee, 1995; Lipsey, 1992; Stumphauzer, 1979).

Cognitive programs. Cognitive restructuring (i.e, changing a juvenile's "self-talk") has produced successful outcomes for several decades. Adolescents, especially juvenile offenders, may have deficits in consequential thinking and alternative thinking. Their thinking is frequently illogical, and they have trouble changing irrational beliefs. Cognitive strategies that address these deficits further the goals of JAIBG by emphasizing accountability and personal responsibility (Agee, 1995; Gibbs et al., 1997; Glick, Sturgeon, and Venator-Santiago, 1998; Lipsey, 1992; Traynelis-Yurek, 1997).

Positive peer cultures. Although positive group dynamics is an important part of successful programs, the ultimate empowerment for youth is having the opportunity to solve their own problems. Researchers have shown that youth are more motivated to behave appropriately when other youth participate in decisionmaking about the intervention. They also gain a greater sense of self-worth when they are able to help themselves and others (Brendtro and Ness, 1983; Ferrara, 1992; Vorrath and Brendtro, 1984; Wasmund, 1988).

Anger management. With violence becoming increasingly common in American society, youth in juvenile confinement facilities are becoming more comfortable using violence as a problem-solving strategy. Anger management, however, can be learned, and it is a prerequisite for meaningful and lasting behavior change among youth who have exhibited violent behavior (American Psychological Association, 1993; Chinn, 1996; Dobbins and Gatowski, 1996).

Discipline. Discipline, a vital part of effective programs, creates character, courage, pride, and integrity. An inescapable part of every juvenile confinement facility, discipline also sets the tone for all other program interventions. Effective discipline programs set high expectations for youth; employ graduated sanctions; emphasize corrective measures; encourage and celebrate appropriate behaviors, achievements, and accomplishments; and help youth to understand that disciplinary procedures are in their own best interest. Effective discipline programs require strong and committed staff members, who must make discipline part of their own lives—not just part of their jobs.

Empathy training. Empathy training (one of the BARJ model's restorative elements) includes helping juveniles become aware of and empathize with their victims. Awareness and empathy are necessary precursors to feelings of guilt, shame, and remorse.

Social skills training. Most juvenile offenders lack adequate social skills. Many do not know how to relate to persons outside their family or gang. Experience indicates that social skills programming is an important part of juvenile detention and corrections programs (Roush, 1998).

Drug and alcohol abuse counseling. Many youth entering juvenile confinement facilities are under the influence of alcohol and/or other drugs or have a history of abusing these substances.

Drug and alcohol counseling programs are therefore important ancillary services that can improve the effectiveness of model programs (Agee, 1995; Cellini, 1994; Howell, 1997).

Transition and aftercare services. Without transition and aftercare programs, changes occurring within an institutional setting are unlikely to have long-lasting effects. Transition programs move youth back into the community gradually. Aftercare involves having a specially trained aftercare worker or probation officer work with youth in the community for an extended period of time (until the youth is comfortable being back in the community or has met a specified set of criteria). As the number of youth in the juvenile justice system has increased, caseloads have become so large that aftercare and parole services officers have insufficient time to address all of the problems of the youth on their caseloads. Therefore, many youth's problems are unaddressed or neglected; without supervision, youth often quickly return to lives of drugs and crime (Agee, 1995; Altschuler and Armstrong, 1995; Howell, 1997; Lipsey, 1992).

When using any of the techniques above, facilities should explain related expectations clearly to each juvenile entering the facility. Expectations should be systematic (use a method to achieve goals); logical (make sense); rigorous (place high expectations on youth for improved performance); and balanced (emphasize strengths while administering sanctions/punishments).

Staffing and management principles

Recruitment, selection, retention, and development of good staff members are strengths of every successful program. Several organizations and individuals have examined the characteristics of effective juvenile justice staff (Glick, Sturgeon, and Venator-Santiago,

1998; Goldstein and Glick, 1987; Previte, 1994; Roush, 1996b). Lists of attributes compiled by researchers have been fairly similar and include such traits as patience, the ability to interact effectively with other people (i.e., social, communication, and relationship skills), cooperation, respect, empathy, the ability to work as a team player, alertness, physical strength, and optimism.

Once a facility hires good staff members, it needs to determine which management principles are linked to best practice operations. Four principles are presented below.[6]

Consistency. Best practice programs have highly consistent management principles. Consistency involves at least three elements.

■ *Rules that provide structure and dependability but do not overwhelm youth.* Rules should be clear and understandable. They should be few in number and general in nature. Realizing that not every misbehavior can be addressed by a specific rule, best practices programs have rules based on general principles (e.g., cooperation, respect, and responsibility). Rules and structure are the backbone of emotional and physical safety and provide the foundation for discipline and self-control in children (Humphrey, 1984). According to Previte (1994), rules are an institution's way of saying "I care" to youth.

■ *Rule enforcement that is firm but fair.* Because adolescents are often concerned with fairness, facilities should enforce rules in a firm and fair manner. While perceptions of unfairness generate feelings of anger and resentment, perceptions of fairness generate cooperation and

increased safety. Being firm but fair means several things. It means that rules are enforced uniformly, with no second chances, excuses, or warnings (unless rules call for a warning). Rules are enforced matter-of-factly, without emotion on the part of staff. The staff member's role is simply to enforce rules, not to provide a lecture, sermon, or interrogation about a youth's knowledge of the rules. Violating a rule is a youth's choice; if the consequences for rule violations have been clearly specified in advance, the youth also chooses the consequence when he or she violates a rule. Being fair also means providing procedures for changing or eliminating unreasonable rules.

■ *A social order.* A facility needs to develop a social order (i.e., consistent rules that govern everyone in the facility, including staff) (Roush, 1984). There will always be two sets of rules—one for staff (including rules that apply to facility operation) and one for residents. Best practices programs, however, have certain rules of conduct that apply to everyone. Such a social order encourages the development of respect and dignity.

Involvement. Involvement means that a program includes activity, interaction, and staff-resident relationships. Regardless of their content, all effective programs are active—with youth in the best programs spending **as many as 14 hours each day in structured and supervised activities** (American Correctional Association, 1991a, 1991c). In addition to being enjoyable, active programs are physically and mentally challenging. They are purposeful, educational, and helpful (Roush, 1993). They are also outlets for youthful energy: youth in active programs are tired and ready to sleep at the end of the day.

Involvement also requires interaction between staff and residents, ranging from active supervision of an activity

(residents are within earshot of or only a few feet away from staff) to actual staff participation in an activity.

The essence of involvement in juvenile facilities is the relationship between residents and staff. Staff members should be involved in juveniles' lives in a constructive way. In the best programs, staff members have chosen their jobs primarily because they like youth and genuinely want to help. Without compromising a facility's structure and order, these staff members listen to the residents, and, as Previte (1994) explains, "Listening creates hope, and hope is power."

Emphasis on positive consequences. Successful programs emphasize the positive (Carrera, 1996). In fact, they use positive consequences at least four times more often than negative sanctions (Madsen, Becker, and Thomas, 1968). Effective programs must be both demanding and encouraging and must communicate both positive and negative messages appropriately, clearly, and without compromise.

To achieve the balance referred to in the BARJ model, juvenile justice practitioners must be open to including positive youth development programs, rather than focusing exclusively on problems, needs, skill deficits, and other "negatives." Matching programs and services to offender needs and deficits may be effective; however, as Karen Pittman of the International Youth Foundation has observed, being problem free is not the same as being fully prepared (1996). A positive approach focusing on the strengths of youth—rather than one focusing solely on their problems or needs—has produced effective outcomes (Brendtro and Ness, 1995; Checkoway and Finn, 1992; Clark, 1995, 1996; Leffert et al., 1996; Seita, Mitchell, and Tobin, 1996). Positive youth development programs that can be used in juvenile confinement facilities include sports and recreation activities, camping programs, service programs, mentoring programs,

---

[6] For more information on management principles and other operations issues, jurisdictions should call the OJJDP National Training and Technical Assistance Center at 800-830-4031. Additional sources of information on operating a juvenile facility also appear at the end of this Bulletin, under "For Further Information."

school-to-work programs, and support for teen parents.

Respect. No management principles will work without respect. Respect means treating juveniles like worthwhile human beings, regardless of their behavior, appearance, offense history, psychological assessment, hygiene, or volatility. It means refraining from name calling, threats, putdowns, and cursing. According to youth, respect is the single most important trait of a good staff member in any type of program. A respectful and nonjudgmental approach separates the deed from the doer, allowing staff to treat youth with respect no matter how reprehensible the youth's conduct may be.

Respect leads staff to focus on similarities (rather than differences) between themselves and the juveniles under their care. For example, when staff of the Utah County Juvenile Detention Center (Provo, UT) were asked to explain their motivation for working with youth in the juvenile justice system, the majority stated, "These are *my* brothers and sisters who are in trouble. I am here to help them."

Juvenile Facility Staff Training

Fundamental Needs

Citing numerous links between inadequate staff training and serious problems (e.g., suicidal behaviors by residents), OJJDP's study on conditions of confinement confirmed the need for additional staff training (Parent et al., 1994). Many problems with conditions of confinement occurred in facilities where staff had deficits in specific knowledge and skill areas. The study also reinforced the belief that juvenile institutions should give priority to improving training for new staff (given the high levels of staff turnover) and adding training for all staff in the areas of adolescent health care, education, treatment, access issues,

juveniles' rights, and limits or controls on staff discretion.

OJJDP's *Juvenile Detention Training Needs Assessment* (Roush, 1996c) identified factors that heighten the need for improved training. These factors include uneven levels of preemployment education among staff, high rates of staff turnover, lateral shifts in personnel, increasingly complex needs of juvenile offenders, worker liability issues, and development of new technologies. According to detention administrators in Michigan, scarce funding was the primary problem facing facilities that wanted to improve training (Michigan Juvenile Detention Association, 1981). More than two-thirds of New Jersey detention facilities did not even have a training budget in 1990 (Lucas, 1991). Juvenile facility staff cite scheduling difficulties (e.g., interruptions in training because of staffing problems and crowding) as the major obstacle to implementing training programs (Brown, 1982; Roush, 1996c).

Staff Training

Even though juvenile facility staff training has made significant progress over the past decade, and access to training information, resources, and services has never been better, training remains one of the highest ranked needs among line staff. One promising sign that training is becoming more widely available is the rapid growth of State-operated training academies: only six such academies existed in 1944, while today more than half of the States operate academies.

The recent overall improvement in staff training is attributable to three factors. First, knowledge about effective training in general has been applied to juvenile justice specifically, resulting in a knowledge base and technology that are specific to juvenile justice system needs (National Training and Technical Assistance Center, 1998; Blair et al., undated; Cellini, 1995; Christy, 1989). Second, professional associations

and organizations—particularly the American Correctional Association (ACA); the Association for Staff Training and Development (ASTD); the Juvenile Justice Trainers Association (JJTA) (a professional organization devoted entirely to training); the National Institute of Corrections (NIC) Academy Division (the training arm of the Federal Bureau of Prisons); and the National Juvenile Detention Association (NJDA)—have expanded the network of skilled trainers. Third, OJJDP has provided strong leadership and support through its Training and Technical Assistance Division. Some of the contributions to training made by ACA, NJDA, JJTA, and OJJDP are described below.

ACA

Through standards that specify an annual minimum number of training hours for each category of employee at various periods in his or her employment, ACA has confirmed the importance of staff training (American Correctional Association, 1991a, 1991c). With facilities' accreditation dependent upon compliance with ACA training standards, comprehensive staff training programs have gained legitimacy, and training funds have increased. What was once thought to be an excessive amount of time for training (160 hours for new employees during their first year) is now generally accepted as a best practice (Roush, 1996c). To sustain this level of training, at least 2 to 4 percent of a facility's annual operations budget should be allocated to staff training services. For more information about accredited juvenile justice facilities, practitioners should contact the ACA Standards and Accreditation Division (800–222–5646) and request a list of facilities, contact persons, and phone numbers.

ACA has also developed useful training materials, including videos and correspondence courses. ACA training videos address topics such as facility admissions, suicide prevention, and cultural diversity. Correspondence courses through ACA address basic careworker skills, behavior management, suicide prevention, and supervision of youthful offenders. Upon successfully completing courses and passing an examination, an employee receives a certificate from ACA.

NJDA

NJDA research (Roush, 1996c) has affirmed ACA's training requirements, identified five discrete training categories for juvenile justice employees, and developed learning objectives to supplement the training topics identified by ACA. Through OJJDP grants, NJDA and JJTA developed and tested two 40-hour training curriculums for line staff in juvenile detention and corrections facilities. The curriculums are based on national training needs assessment data (Roush and Jones, 1996), and the lesson plans developed follow the Instructional Theory Into Practice (ITIP) model recommended by NIC. NJDA also has developed a training implementation model intended to strengthen and expand facilities' in-house training capabilities (Roush, 1996a). Through the use of the Training Needs Assessment Inventory (TNAI) and interchangeable lesson plans, institutions can tailor training interventions to meet their specific needs.

JJTA

With the development of *Guidelines for Quality Training* (Blair et al., undated) and *OJJDP Training, Technical Assistance, and Evaluation Protocols: A Primer for OJJDP Training and Technical Assistance Providers* (National Training and Technical Assistance Center, 1998), JJTA has provided basic information about the necessary components of a model staff training program. Composed primarily of staff development and training specialists, JJTA provides a national network of information on training services and technical assistance for juvenile justice trainers.

NIC has also developed a 27-step training implementation strategy. Combined with *Training, Technical Assistance, and Evaluation Protocols: A Primer for OJJDP Training and Technical Assistance Providers*, this strategy provides sufficient knowledge to generate a comprehensive staff training program. Facilities can secure information on the entire network of resources available by referring to the *Training and Technical Assistance Resource Catalog*, updated and published annually by the National Training and Technical Assistance Center, or by calling the center at 800–830–4031.

OJJDP

In 1990, OJJDP entered into an interagency agreement with the NIC Academy Division to provide leadership development programs for juvenile detention and corrections personnel. Under the agreement, NIC offers correctional leadership development (CLD) programs for new chief executive officers, managers, and supervisors. OJJDP produced a video on leadership in juvenile justice based on NIC's leadership development curriculum. NIC's training-for-trainers workshop, which uses the ITIP model, is rated by juvenile justice practitioners as one of the best programs for developing foundation skills for trainers. OJJDP also provides technical assistance resources for line staff training through NJDA's Center for Research and Professional Development (517–432–1242) and for management staff training through the NIC Academy Division (800–995–6429).

Six Major Steps to Implementation

Several important steps must be completed to construct a model staff training program. As in the master planning process, a facility should begin by articulating vision and mission statements. The subsequent steps are described below.

Step 1: Conduct a training needs assessment

A facility should first conduct a training needs assessment to identify gaps between the knowledge, skills, and abilities needed to perform jobs effectively and the knowledge, skills, and abilities currently possessed by staff members. The larger the gap, the greater the training need. Assessment instruments and procedures can be used to collect this information, and juvenile justice trainers are available to conduct needs assessments for agencies and organizations.

Step 2: Develop a formal training plan

Based on information revealed by its needs assessment, a facility should formalize its training strategy. This strategy generally takes the form of training policies and procedures in which the facility identifies who the trainers will be, what types of training will be offered, which staff members will be trained, and how many hours of training are to be provided annually for each position. Training policies and procedures should also establish minimum training requirements for staff at different levels and identify any administrative, professional, and/or statutory standards or requirements that the facility will meet.

Step 3: Adopt, adapt, or develop a core curriculum

Based on the training needs identified and the training plan developed, a facility should adopt, adapt, or develop a core curriculum as its primary training vehicle. Several curriculums are available, including three developed by OJJDP grants: the National Detention Careworker Curriculum, the Juvenile Corrections Careworker Curriculum, and the National Training Curriculum for Educators in Juvenile Confinement Facilities. To obtain copies of these curriculums, practitioners should contact NJDA, listed in the "For Further Information" section.

Step 4: Adopt an action strategy

A facility should next adopt an action strategy for delivering training services. As discussed above, a majority of States have training academies responsible for training all personnel in State-operated juvenile correctional and detention facilities. Facilities not covered by a State training academy are responsible for devising their own training delivery strategies.

Responding to the need for a training delivery strategy for locally operated juvenile facilities and facilities in States without training academies, NJDA developed and tested a training implementation strategy. NJDA's strategy includes developing vision and mission statements, conducting a training needs assessment, developing a formal training plan, and selecting a training curriculum. NJDA's strategy also addresses identification of key staff members (middle managers, shift supervisors, and lead workers) to serve as staff trainers. After completing a basic training curriculum in a separate training workshop, these key staff members are divided into two groups: trainers and mentors. Trainers complete a 40-hour program on building training foundation skills using the NIC model. Mentors (those key staff who do not want or should not have staff training responsibilities) receive training on mentoring so that they can help guide new employees through the training process. The NJDA strategy has proven successful in strengthening in-house training capabilities.

Step 5: Schedule training

The next major step is to schedule training, a task that is extremely difficult when a facility lacks sufficient resources to provide coverage for staff members attending training. The NJDA makes scheduling easier by expanding the cadre of in-house staff trainers.

Several scheduling strategies have been successful. The Cook County Temporary Juvenile Detention Center (Chicago, IL), for example, has a full-time training staff devoted to organizing and delivering training services that meet ACA standards. To improve ongoing training efforts, particularly in-service training, at the Bexar County Juvenile Detention Center (San Antonio, TX), Kossman (1990) implemented an innovative, four-shift staffing pattern. Instead of the routine three-shift (a.m., p.m., and night) scheduling assignments, he added a fourth shift as a replacement for those shifts attending staff training. Using the four-shift pattern, Kossman reported reductions in overtime costs and a greater commitment to training.

Step 6: Evaluate training

As a final step, facilities should evaluate training. Evaluations should include trainees' reactions and suggestions for improvement and plans or commitments to implement training lessons in daily practice. Facilities should conduct evaluations on an ongoing basis to determine whether staff behavior and institutional practices have changed as a result of training and whether the direction of any change is compatible with the goals of training. Results of evaluation efforts also provide information about the nature and extent of a facility's training needs. This information, in turn, becomes data for training needs assessment. The process has now come full circle, with evaluation data guiding future training needs assessment, annual revisions and modifications to the training plan, and updates to a facility's training curriculum.

Conclusion

Even though extensive literature on juvenile justice exists, best practices are difficult to define (Elliot, 1998). The purpose of this Bulletin is not to prescribe a specific best practice. Rather, it seeks to identify resources (especially knowledge, principles, and people) that can inform practitioners, policymakers, and the public in their quest to develop and implement best practices in the areas of juvenile facility construction, operations, and staff training. This is really a search for "best knowledge"; once this knowledge is located, best practice is not far behind.

It is often easier to ascertain best practices in the area of construction because the physical structures that result are available for a wide array of examination and analysis. This is not always the case when searching for best practices in the areas of operations and staff training. In these areas, the search for models and examples of best practice is most productive when it begins with people—as opposed to places. Best practice is found through best practitioners.

There has never been a better time to acquire knowledge from practitioners. The expansion of juvenile justice has brought many new and talented people into the field. Communication technologies are also better than ever. Professional organizations (including the Alliance for Juvenile Justice, the American Correctional Association, the American Probation and Parole Association, the Council of Juvenile Corrections Administrators, the Juvenile Justice Trainers Association, the National Association of Juvenile Correctional Agencies, the National Council of Juvenile and Family Court Judges, the National Council on Crime and Delinquency, the National Juvenile Court Services Association, and the National Juvenile Detention Association) offer access to abundant information, resources, and personal contacts. The excuses for *not* knowing are rapidly disappearing.

References

Agee, V.M. 1995. Managing clinical programs for juvenile delinquents. In *Managing Delinquency Programs That Work,* edited by B. Glick and A.P. Goldstein. Laurel, MD: American Correctional Association.

Altschuler, D.M., and Armstrong, T.L. 1995. Managing aftercare services for delinquents. In *Managing Delinquency Programs That Work,* edited by B. Glick and A.P. Goldstein. Laurel, MD: American Correctional Association.

American Correctional Association. 1987. *Admissions in Juvenile Detention: The Critical Hour.* Videotape. Washington, DC: Capitol Communication Systems, Inc.

American Correctional Association. 1991a. *Standards for Juvenile Detention Facilities,* 3d ed. Laurel, MD: American Correctional Association.

American Correctional Association. 1991b. *Standards for Juvenile Training Schools,* 3d ed. Laurel, MD: American Correctional Association.

American Correctional Association. 1991c. *Standards for Small Juvenile Detention Facilities.* Laurel, MD: American Correctional Association.

American Correctional Association. 1992a. *Guidelines for the Development of Policies and Procedures: Juvenile Detention Facilities.* Laurel, MD: American Correctional Association.

American Correctional Association. 1992b. *Handbook on Facility Planning and Design for Juvenile Corrections.* Laurel, MD: American Correctional Association.

American Correctional Association. 1992c. *Juvenile Careworker Resource Guide.* Laurel, MD: American Correctional Association.

American Correctional Association. 1994. *1994 Standards Supplement.* Laurel, MD: American Correctional Association.

American Psychological Association Commission on Violence and Youth. 1993. *Violence and Youth: Psychology's Response.* Washington, DC: American Psychological Association.

Barrueta-Clement, J.R., Schweinhart, L.J., Barnett, W.S., Epstein, A., and Weikart, D. 1984. *Changed Lives: The*

Effects of the Perry Preschool Program on Youth Through Age 19. Ypsilanti, MI: High/Scope Educational Research Foundation.

Barton, W.H. 1994. Implementing detention policy changes. In *Reforming Juvenile Detention: No More Hidden Closets,* edited by I.M. Schwartz and W.H. Barton. Columbus, OH: Ohio State University Press.

Bell, J.R. 1990. Litigation in juvenile justice: A tool for advancement. *Corrections Today* (August):22–23, 26, 28.

Bell, J.R. 1992. Rights and responsibilities of juveniles. In *Juvenile Careworker Resource Guide.* Laurel, MD: American Correctional Association.

Bell, J.R. 1996. Rights and responsibilities of staff and youth. In *Desktop Guide to Good Juvenile Detention Practice,* edited by D.W. Roush. Washington, DC: U.S. Department of Justice, Office of Justice Programs, Office of Juvenile Justice and Delinquency Prevention.

Bell, J.R. 1998. National perspectives on juvenile justice. Keynote address to the American Institute of Architecture Conference.

Bilchik, S. 1998. *A Juvenile Justice System for the 21st Century.* Bulletin. Washington, DC: U.S. Department of Justice, Office of Justice Programs, Office of Juvenile Justice and Delinquency Prevention.

Blair, J., Collins, B., Gurnell, B., Satterfield, F., Smith, M.G., Yeres, S., and Zuercher, R. Undated. *Guidelines for Quality Training.* Ithaca, NY: Juvenile Justice Trainers Association.

Boersema, C. 1998. Strategic planning as a means to address detention overcrowding. *Journal for Juvenile Justice and Detention Services* 13(Spring):20–31.

Boersema, C., Dunlap, E., Gulley, J., and Roush, D.W. 1997. *Juvenile Justice System Master Plan for Detention Services: Final Report.* Richmond, KY: National Juvenile Detention Association.

Brendtro, L.K., and Ness, A.E. 1983. *Re-educating Troubled Youth: Environments for Teaching and Treatment.* New York, NY: Aldine Publishing.

Brendtro, L.K., and Ness, A.E. 1995. Fixing flaws or building strengths? *Reclaiming Children and Youth* 4:2–7.

Brown, M., Jr. 1982. Training officers in juvenile detention. *Corrections Today* (June):14–16, 18.

Burrell, S., DeMuro, P., Dunlap, E., Sanniti, C., and Warboys, L. 1998. *Crowding in Juvenile Detention Centers: A Problem-Solving Manual.* Washington, DC: U.S. Department of Justice, Office of Justice Programs, Office of Juvenile Justice and Delinquency Prevention.

Butterfield, F. 1998. Hard times: Profits at a juvenile prison come with a chilling cost. *The New York Times on the Web* (July 15):1–17.

Calloway, J. 1995. Managing recreation and leisure for juvenile delinquents. In *Managing Delinquency Programs That Work,* edited by B. Glick and A.P. Goldstein. Laurel, MD: American Correctional Association.

Carrera, M.A. 1996. *Lessons for Lifeguards: Working with Teens When the Topic Is Hope.* NewYork, NY: Donkey Press.

Cavanagh, M.F. 1995. Remarks. *Journal for Juvenile Justice and Detention Services* 10(Fall):37–40.

Cellini, H.R. 1994. Management and treatment of institutionalized violent juveniles. *Corrections Today* (July):98, 100–102.

Cellini, H.R. 1995. Training programs and staff development. In *Managing Delinquency Programs That Work,* edited by B. Glick and A.P. Goldstein. Laurel, MD: American Correctional Association.

Checkoway, B., and Finn, J. 1992. *Young People as Community Builders.* Ann Arbor, MI: Center for the Study of Youth Policy, University of Michigan.

Chinn, K.L. 1996. National trends in juvenile violence. *Corrections Today* (July):70, 72–73.

Christy, J.T. 1989. A curriculum for training juvenile detention staff. *Journal for Juvenile Justice and Detention Services* 4(Winter):23–29.

Christy, J.T. 1994. Toward a model secure detention program: Lessons from Shuman Center. In *Reforming Juvenile Detention: No More Hidden Closets,* edited by I.M. Schwartz and W. Barton. Columbus, OH: Ohio State University Press.

Clark, M.D. 1995. The problem with problem solving: A critical review. *Journal for Juvenile Justice and Detention Services* 10(Spring):30–35.

Clark, M.D. 1996. Solution-focused interviewing: A strength-based method for juvenile justice. *Journal for Juvenile Justice and Detention Services* 11(Spring):33–38.

Cocozza, J.J., ed. 1992. *Responding to the Mental Health Needs of Youth in the Juvenile Justice System.* Seattle, WA: National Coalition for the Mentally Ill in the Criminal Justice System.

Coordinating Council on Juvenile Justice and Delinquency Prevention. 1996. *Combating Violence and Delinquency: The National Juvenile Justice Action Plan.* Washington, DC: U.S. Department of Justice, Office of Justice Programs, Office of Juvenile Justice and Delinquency Prevention.

DeMuro, P. 1997. Overcrowding in juvenile detention: Some concrete suggestions. *Texas Probation* 12(July):11–17.

DeMuro, P., and Dunlap, E.L. 1998. A reasonable alternative to locking up more kids: The development of jurisdictional core groups. *Journal for Juvenile Justice and Detention Services* 13(Spring):3–19.

DeWitt, C.B. 1987. *Building on Experience: A Case Study of Advanced Construction and Financing Methods for Corrections.* Washington, DC: U.S.

Department of Justice, Office of Justice Programs, National Institute of Corrections.

Dobbins, S.A., and Gatowski, S.I. 1996. *A Guide to Research on Juvenile Violence.* Reno, NV: State Judicial Institute and the National Council of Juvenile and Family Court Judges.

Dugan, R.J. 1998. A juvenile detention facility that works. In *Best Practices: Excellence in Corrections,* edited by E. Rhine. Lanham, MD: American Correctional Association.

Dunlap, E.L., and Roush, D.W. 1995. Juvenile detention as process and place. *Juvenile and Family Court Journal* 46(Spring):3–16.

Elias, G.L., and Ricci, K. 1997. *Woman in Jail: Facility Planning Issues.* Washington, DC: U.S. Department of Justice, Office of Justice Programs, National Institute of Corrections.

Elliot, D.E. 1998. What makes a "best practice"? In *Proceedings of the 1998 Governor's Juvenile Justice Summit.* Columbus, OH: Office of Criminal Justice Services.

Farbstein, J., Liebert, D., and Sigurdson, H. 1996. *Audits of Podular Direct-Supervision Jails.* Washington, DC: U.S. Department of Justice, Office of Justice Programs, National Institute of Corrections.

Farbstein/Williams and Associates. 1981. *Corrections Planning Handbooks.* Sacramento, CA: California Board of Corrections, Youth and Adult Correctional Agency.

Ferrara, M.L. 1992. *Group Counseling with Juvenile Delinquents: The Limit and Lead Approach.* Newbury Park, CA: Sage Publications, Inc.

Gemignani, R.J. 1994. *Juvenile Correctional Education: A Time for Change.* OJJDP Update on Research. Bulletin. Washington, DC: U.S. Department of Justice, Office of Justice Programs, Office of Juvenile Justice and Delinquency Prevention.

Gibbs, J., Potter, B., Goldstein, A., and Brendtro, L. 1997. Equipping youth to think and act constructively. *Reclaiming Children and Youth: Journal of Emotional and Behavioral Problems* 6(Summer):120–127.

Glick, B., and Goldstein, A.P., eds. 1995. *Managing Delinquency Programs That Work.* Laurel, MD: American Correctional Association.

Glick, B., Sturgeon, W., and Venator-Santiago, C.R. 1998. *No Time to Play: Youthful Offenders in Adult Correctional Systems.* Lanham, MD: American Correctional Association.

Goldstein, A.P., and Glick, B. 1987. *Aggression Replacement Training: A Comprehensive Intervention for Aggressive Youth.* Champaign, IL: Research Press.

Grimm, R. 1998. Is there life after basketball? Presentation to the 18th Annual Governor's Conference on Juvenile Justice, New Orleans, LA.

Guarino-Ghezzi, S., and Loughran, E.J. 1996. *Balancing Juvenile Justice.* New Brunswick, NJ: Transaction Publishers.

Hayes, L.M. 1998. Suicide prevention in correctional facilities: An overview. In *Clinical Practice in Correctional Medicine,* edited by M. Puisis. St. Louis, MO: Mosby.

Henggeler, S.W. 1998. *Treating Serious Anti-Social Behavior in Youth: The MST Approach.* Bulletin. Washington, DC: U.S. Department of Justice, Office of Justice Programs, Office of Juvenile Justice and Delinquency Prevention.

Hodges, J., Giuliotti, N., and Porpotage, F.M., II. 1994. *Improving Literacy Skills of Juvenile Detainees.* Bulletin. Washington, DC: U.S. Department of Justice, Office of Justice Programs, Office of Juvenile Justice and Delinquency Prevention.

Howell, J.C., ed. 1995a. *Guide for Implementing the Comprehensive Strategy for Serious, Violent, and Chronic Juvenile Offenders.* Summary. Washington, DC: U.S. Department of Justice,

Office of Justice Programs, Office of Juvenile Justice and Delinquency Prevention.

Howell, J.C. 1995b. A national perspective. In *Managing Delinquency Programs That Work,* edited by B. Glick and A.P. Goldstein. Laurel, MD: American Correctional Association.

Howell, J.C. 1997. *Juvenile Justice and Youth Violence.* Thousand Oaks, CA: Sage Publications, Inc.

Howell, J.C., Krisberg, B., Hawkins, J.D., and Wilson, J.J., eds. 1995. *Serious, Violent, and Chronic Juvenile Offenders: A Sourcebook.* Thousand Oaks, CA: Sage Publications, Inc.

Humphrey, L.L. 1984. Children's self-control in relation to perceived social environment. *Journal of Personality and Social Psychology* 46:178–188.

Jones, M.A., and Krisberg, B. 1994. *Images and Reality: Juvenile Crime, Youth Violence, and Public Policy.* San Francisco, CA: National Council on Crime and Delinquency.

Jones, M.A., and Steinhart, D. 1994. Assessing the need for secure detention: A planning approach. *NCCD Focus* (August):1–7.

Kearns, R. 1998. No profit for kids in Glen Mills' Florida plunge. *Youth Today* 7(June):1, 37–38.

Kimme, D.A., Bowker, G., Deichman, R., Bounds, B., Reisteck, C., and Farbstein, J. 1988. *Small Jail Design Guide: A Planning and Design Resource for Local Facilities of Up to 50 Beds.* Washington, D.C.: U.S. Department of Justice, Office of Justice Programs, National Institute of Corrections.

Kossman, S.P. 1990. Staffing pattern dynamics: A new approach to old problems. *Journal for Juvenile Justice and Detention Services* 5(Fall):9–12.

Kostelnik, M.J., Soderman, A.K., and Whiren, A.P. 1999. *Developmentally Appropriate Curriculum: Best Practices in Early Childhood Education.* Upper Saddle River, NJ: Merrill.

Leffert, N., Saito, R.N., Blyth, D.A., and Kroenke, C.H. 1996. *Making the Case: Measuring the Impact of Youth Development Programs.* Minneapolis, MN: The Search Institute.

Leone, P.E., Rutherford, R.B., and Nelson, C.M. 1991. *Special Education in Juvenile Corrections.* Reston, VA: Council for Exceptional Children.

Lipsey, M.W. 1992. Juvenile delinquency treatment: A meta-analytic inquiry into the variability of effects. In *Meta-Analysis for Explanation: A Casebook,* edited by T.D. Cook, H. Cooper, and D.S. Cordray. New York, NY: Russell Sage Foundation.

Lucas, C. 1991. *Juvenile Detention Staff Development Initiative: Survey of Training Resources.* Trenton, NJ: New Jersey Department of Corrections.

Madsen. C.H., Becker, W.C., and Thomas, D.R. 1968. Rules, praise, and ignoring: Elements of elementary classroom control. *Journal of Applied Behavior Analysis* 1:139–150.

McMillen, M. 1998. Planning juvenile detention facilities: The *real* costs. *Journal for Juvenile Justice and Detention Services* 13(Spring):49–57.

McMillen, M., and Hill, J.R. 1997. Jadults and adulniles. *Corrections Today* (April):100–101, 102–104.

Michigan Juvenile Detention Association. 1981. *Child Care Staff Training: Two Unresolved Issues.* Marshall, MI: Michigan Juvenile Detention Association.

Mitchell, J., and Varley, C. 1991. Isolation and restraint in juvenile correctional facilities. *Journal for Juvenile Justice and Detention Services* 6(Fall):31–37.

Moon, M.M., Applegate, B.K., and Latessa, E.J. 1997. RECLAIM Ohio: A politically viable alternative to treating youthful felony offenders. *Crime & Delinquency* 43(October):438–456.

Morris, R., Anderson, M., and Baker, C. 1996. Health care for incarcerated adolescents. In *Desktop Guide to Good Juvenile Detention Practice,* edited by

D.W. Roush. Washington, DC: U.S. Department of Justice, Office of Justice Programs, Office of Juvenile Justice and Delinquency Prevention.

National Clearinghouse for Criminal Justice Planning and Architecture. 1996. Criminal justice planning process: A total systems model. *Planning of New Institutions Workshops.* Longmont, CO: National Institute of Corrections.

National Commission on Correctional Health Care. 1999. *Standards for Health Services in Juvenile Detention and Confinement Facilities.* Chicago, IL: National Commission on Correctional Health Care.

National Commission on Correctional Health Care. 1998. Health services to adolescents in adult correctional facilities: Position statement. *Journal of Correctional Health Care* 5(Spring):113–117.

National Training and Technical Assistance Center. 1998. *OJJDP Training and Technical Assistance Protocols: A Primer for OJJDP Training and Technical Assistance Providers.* Washington, DC: U.S. Department of Justice, Office of Justice Programs, Office of Juvenile Justice and Delinquency Prevention.

Nelson, W.R. 1993. New generation jails. In *Podular Direct Supervision Jails.* Washington, DC: U.S. Department of Justice, National Institute of Corrections, Jails Division.

Nelson, W.R., O'Toole, M., Krauth, B., and Whitmore, C.G. 1984. *Direct Supervision Models.* Boulder, CO: National Institute of Corrections Information Center.

Niedringhous, R.T., and Goedert, P. 1998. New rules in juvenile justice design. *Corrections Today* (February): 58–60.

Norman, S., ed. 1961. *Standards and Guides for the Detention of Children and Youth,* 2d ed. New York, NY: National Council on Crime and Delinquency.

Office of Juvenile Justice and Delinquency Prevention. 1998. *1997 Report to Congress: Title V Incentive Grants for*

Local Delinquency Prevention Programs. Report. Washington, DC: U.S. Department of Justice, Office of Justice Programs, Office of Juvenile Justice and Delinquency Prevention.

Otto, R.K., Greenstein, J.J., Johnson, M.K., and Friedman, R.M. 1992. Prevalence of mental disorders among youth in the juvenile justice system. In *Responding to the Mental Health Needs of Youth in the Juvenile Justice System,* edited by J.J. Cocozza. Seattle, WA: National Coalition for the Mentally Ill in the Criminal Justice System.

Owens, J. 1994. Juvenile health care in correctional facilities: A public health opportunity. *New York Health Services Journal* 1(Spring):55–66.

Parent, D., Leiter, V., Kennedy, S., Livens, L., Wentworth, D., and Wilcox, S. 1994. *Conditions of Confinement: Juvenile Detention and Corrections Facilities.* Research Report. Washington, DC: U.S. Department of Justice, Office of Justice Programs, Office of Juvenile Justice and Delinquency Prevention.

Pittman, K.J. 1996. Community, youth, development: Three goals in search of connection. *New Designs for Youth Development* (Winter).

Previte, M.T. 1994. *Hungry Ghosts: One Woman's Mission to Change Their World.* Grand Rapids, MI: Zondervan Publishing House.

Previte, M.T. 1997. Preventing security crises at youth centers. *Corrections Today* (February):76–79.

Puritz, P., and Scali, M.A. 1998. *Beyond the Walls: Improving Conditions of Confinement for Youth in Custody.* Report. Washington, DC: U.S. Department of Justice, Office of Justice Programs, Office of Juvenile Justice and Delinquency Prevention.

Ricci, K. 1995. What county commissioners can do about overcrowding in their jails. *The Prison Journal* 61:1–3.

Roush, D.W. 1984. Contributions to the therapeutic milieu: Integrating key theoretical constructs. *Child Care Quarterly* 13:233–250.

Roush, D.W. 1993. Juvenile detention programming. *Federal Probation* 57(September):20–33.

Roush, D.W. 1994. Admission to juvenile detention. *Journal for Juvenile Justice and Detention Services* 9(Fall):32–39.

Roush, D.W. 1996a. A comprehensive strategy for implementing the NJDA careworker training curriculum. *JERITT Bulletin* 7(2):1–4.

Roush, D.W., ed. 1996b. *Desktop Guide to Good Juvenile Detention Practice.* Washington, DC: U.S. Department of Justice, Office of Justice Programs, Office of Juvenile Justice and Delinquency Prevention.

Roush, D.W. 1996c. *Juvenile Detention Training Needs Assessment.* Report. Washington, DC: U.S. Department of Justice, Office of Justice Programs, Office of Juvenile Justice and Delinquency Prevention.

Roush, D.W. 1997. Staffing patterns in juvenile detention facilities. *Journal for Juvenile Justice and Detention Services* 12(Fall):87–94.

Roush, D.W. 1998. The importance of comprehensive skills-based programs in juvenile detention and corrections. In *Juvenile Justice: Policies, Programs and Services,* 2d ed., edited by A.R. Roberts. New York, NY: Nelson-Hall Publishing Company.

Roush, D.W. 1999. Crowding and its effects. In *Juvenile Detention Centers: Applied Resources Manual,* edited by D.W. Roush. Richmond, KY: National Juvenile Detention Association.

Roush, D.W., and Jones, M.A. 1996. Juvenile detention training: A status report. *Federal Probation* 60(June):54–60.

Rowan, J.R. 1989. Suicide detection and prevention: A must for juvenile facilities. *Corrections Today* (August):218, 219, 226–227.

Rubenstein, F.D. 1991. A facility-wide approach to social skills training. *Journal of Correctional Education* 42(June):88–93.

Schwartz, I.M. 1994. What policymakers need to know about juvenile detention reform. In *Reforming Juvenile Detention: No More Hidden Closets,* edited by I.M. Schwartz and W.H. Barton. Columbus, OH: Ohio State University Press.

Seita, J., Mitchell, M., and Tobin, C. 1996. *In Whose Best Interest? One Child's Odyssey, a Nation's Responsibility.* Elizabethtown, NJ: Continental Press.

Soler, M.I., Shotton, A., Bell, J., Jameson, E., Shauffer, C., and Warboys, L. 1990. *Representing the Child Client.* New York, NY: Matthew Bender.

Steenson, D., and Thomas, D. 1997. Managing change through strategic planning. In *Juvenile Probation Administrators' Desktop Guide,* edited by D. Thomas and P. Torbet. Pittsburgh, PA: National Center for Juvenile Justice.

Stumphauzer, J.S., ed. 1979. *Progress in Behavior Therapy with Delinquents.* Springfield, IL: Charles C. Thomas, Publisher.

Taylor, J., Gottheil, D., Kimme, D., Bishop, K., and Maase, D. 1996. Seven steps to plan a better jail. In *Planning of New Institutions Workshops.* Longmont, CO: National Institute of Corrections.

Traynelis-Yurek, E. 1997. Thinking clearly through positive peer culture. *Reclaiming Children and Youth: Journal of Emotional and Behavioral Problems* 6(Summer):87–89.

Treahy, J. 1995. Detention services for juveniles. In *Managing Delinquency Programs That Work,* edited by B. Glick and A.P. Goldstein. Laurel, MD: American Correctional Association.

Voorhis, D.J. 1996. The seven stumbling blocks to effective jail planning. In *Planning of New Institutions Workshops.* Longmont, CO: National Institute of Corrections.

Vorrath, H., and Brendtro, L. 1984. *Positive peer culture,* 2d ed. New York, NY: Aldine Publishing.

Wasmund, W.C. 1988. The social climates of peer group and other residential programs. *Child & Youth Care Quarterly* 17(Fall):146–155.

Wilson, J.J., and Howell, J.C. 1993. *Comprehensive Strategy for Serious, Violent, and Chronic Juvenile Offenders.* Summary. Washington, DC: U.S. Department of Justice, Office of Justice Programs, Office of Juvenile Justice and Delinquency Prevention.

Wolford, B.I., and Koebel, L.L. 1995. Reform education to reduce juvenile delinquency. *Criminal Justice* (Winter):2–6, 54–56.

Wright, K.N., and Goodstein, L. 1989. Correctional environments. In *The American Prison: Issues in Research and Policy,* edited by L. Goodstein and D.L. MacKenzie. New York, NY: Plenum Press.

For Further Information

The following sources of information may be helpful before beginning the search for best knowledge and best practices relating to juvenile facility operations:

- American Correctional Association (800–222–5646) has assembled and published information on a variety of best practices.

- American Institute of Architects (202–626–7300), through its library, archives, and online services, is the preeminent source of information in the United States on the practice and profession of architecture.

- The Juvenile Justice Clearinghouse (JJC) (800–638–8736) supplies information to the field through the dissemination of publications, monographs, and reports. Clearinghouse staff provide some research services. Information relevant to best knowledge and practices includes OJJDP publications describing its Gould/Wysinger Award recipients.

- The National Council of Juvenile and Family Court Judges (702–784–6012) has developed curriculum materials that explain many best practices concepts.

- The National Criminal Justice Reference Service (NCJRS) (800–851–3420) will conduct a computer search of relevant criminal and juvenile justice literature.

- The National Institute of Corrections Academy Division (800–995–6429) develops curriculum materials that explain many best practices concepts.

- The National Juvenile Detention Association (517–432–1242) has collected information on innovative programs and services for juvenile detention.

- OJJDP's National Training and Technical Assistance Center (NTTAC) (800–830–4031) has information on individuals, agencies, associations, and grant recipients that address best practices in operations.

- OJJDP's JAIBG Technical Assistance Development Services Group (877–GO–JAIBG) provides and coordinates technical assistance within the 12 JAIBG purpose areas.

Useful Publications

The following guides, handbooks, and manuals provide valuable information on the construction and operation of juvenile detention and corrections facilities:

- *Best Practices: Excellence in Corrections,* a 1998 compilation of best practices, edited by E. Rhine and published by the American Correctional Association.

- *Conflict Resolution Education: A Guide to Implementing Programs in Schools, Youth-Serving Organizations, and Community and Juvenile Justice Settings,* a 1996 guidebook edited by D. Crawford and R. Bodine and published by OJJDP.

- *A Directory of Programs That Work,* a 1996 directory compiled by the American Correctional Association and published in the August 1996 issue of *Corrections.*

- *Effective and Innovative Programs: Resource Manual,* a 1994 manual developed by the National Juvenile Detention Association and edited by D. Roush and T. Wyss.

- *OJJDP Training and Technical Assistance Protocols: A Primer for OJJDP Training and Technical Assistance,* a 1998 collection of protocols compiled by the National Training and Technical Assistance Center and published by OJJDP.

- *Training and Technical Assistance Resource Catalog,* a 1997 catalog of resources compiled by the National Training and Technical Assistance Center and published by OJJDP.

- *What Works: Promising Interventions in Juvenile Justice,* a 1994 manual published by OJJDP and edited by I. Montgomery, P.M. Torbet, D.A. Malloy, L.P. Adamcik, M.J. Toner, and J. Andrews.

Acknowledgments

This Bulletin was written by David Roush, Ph.D., and Michael McMillen, AIA. David Roush has provided leadership in institutional programs and services for juveniles and staff since 1971. He is currently an assistant professor in the School of Criminal Justice at Michigan State University and Director of the National Juvenile Detention Association's Center for Research and Professional Development. Mike McMillen, Champaign, IL, has specialized in the design and planning of juvenile justice facilities for more than 23 years. In addition to providing operations analysis, architectural programming, and facility design services for youth-related projects nationwide, he has developed and currently teaches seminars on operational and architectural programming for the National Institute of Corrections' Planning of New Institutions for Juveniles (PONI) training program.

Points of view or opinions expressed in this document are those of the authors and do not necessarily represent the official position or policies of OJJDP or the U.S. Department of Justice.

The Office of Juvenile Justice and Delinquency Prevention is a component of the Office of Justice Programs, which also includes the Bureau of Justice Assistance, the Bureau of Justice Statistics, the National Institute of Justice, and the Office for Victims of Crime.

Share With Your Colleagues

Unless otherwise noted, OJJDP publications are not copyright protected. We encourage you to reproduce this document, share it with your colleagues, and reprint it in your newsletter or journal. However, if you reprint, please cite OJJDP and the authors of this Bulletin. We are also interested in your feedback, such as how you received a copy, how you intend to use the information, and how OJJDP materials meet your individual or agency needs. Please direct your comments and questions to: